Strategies to score your first few billion dollars

A playbook detailing the strategies and accomplishments of notable contemporary American entrepreneurs.

KELVIN A. WEALTH

TABLE OF CONTENTS

The Mindset of Financial Titans
Spotting Hidden Opportunities
Navigating Economic Shifts

CHAPTER 5

Building a Powerful Network
The Power of Connections: More than Just Handshakes
Strategies for Effective Networking
Cultivating Meaningful Partnerships

CHAPTER 6

Strategic Negotiations
The Symphony of Negotiation
Mastering the Chessboard of Negotiation Strategies
The Art of Silence: A Powerful Negotiation Tool
Negotiation as Relationship Building

CHAPTER 7

THE POWER OF BRANDING
The Branding Symphony
Harmony in Colors, Logos, and Narratives
Branding Beyond Sight: It's a Feeling
From Products to Phenomena
Strategy, Storytelling, and Symbols: The Holy Trinity of Branding
Consumer Loyalty: The Golden Fleece of Branding
Taking Brands Beyond Borders
Navigating Skepticism
The Branding Symphony

CHAPTER 8

Adaptability in a changing world
The Resilient Navigator: A Lesson from Jeff Bezos

CONCLUSION

INTRODUCTION

Welcome to the exhilarating journey outlined in "Strategies to Score Your First Few Billion Dollars." In this captivating playbook, we're about to embark on a whimsical exploration of the business realm, guided by the ingenious insights of some of America's greatest contemporary entrepreneurs. So, fasten your seatbelts, as we navigate the labyrinth of success with a dash of playfulness and a sprinkle of strategic brilliance.

Picture this book as a treasure map, and each chapter unfolds like a hidden gem waiting to be discovered in the vast landscape of wealth creation. The subtitle hints at the playful strategies that will soon become your allies in pursue of those coveted billions—a feat not only reserved for the serious suits but also for those who dare to infuse a bit of play into the high-stakes game of entrepreneurship. Now, you might wonder, what makes this playbook stand out? It's not just a compilation of mundane advice or cookie-cutter strategies. Instead, it's a vibrant mosaic painted with strokes of wit, wisdom, and the unique flavors of America's contemporary entrepreneurial brilliance. Through real-life stories, you'll find yourself immersed in a narrative that not only educates but entertains, turning the pursuit of billions into an exciting and enjoyable adventure.

As we unravel the pages of this playbook, you'll discover that making billions isn't a dry, monotone process; it's a symphony of creativity, resilience, and strategic play. Whether you're a seasoned entrepreneur or just starting your journey, the playful strategies within these chapters will open your eyes to a world where success is not just measured in dollars, but in the journey's joy.

Imagine sitting down for a cup of coffee with some of America's greatest contemporary entrepreneurs—a casual yet profound conversation where you glean the secrets of their success, peppered with laughter and unexpected revelations. That's the essence of this book. It's not a stern lecture; it's a lively conversation that invites you to step into the minds of visionaries who've not only cracked the code of wealth but have done so with a playful twinkle in their eye.

So, let's dive into the heart of this compelling playbook, where billion-dollar strategies unfold with the charm of a well-played game. Get ready to absorb, apply, and perhaps even challenge these guidelines, turning your pursuit of billions into an enjoyable venture. After all, who said making billions can't be a playful affair? Let the journey begin!

Chapter1

Unleashing the Entrepreneurial Spirit

Welcome, fellow dreamers and doers, to the gateway of your journey into the exhilarating world of entrepreneurship. Strap in for an expedition of self-discovery, where the air resonates with the fragrance of possibility and the landscape is adorned with opportunities ready to be seized. In the grand tapestry of wealth creation, entrepreneurship orchestrates the masterstroke—a symphony of innovation, resilience, and vision. Picture it as your golden ticket to the Willy Wonka factory of financial success. But before you sprint towards that metaphorical chocolate river, let's lay down the foundational principles that will be your compass through this entrepreneurial odyssey.

Identifying Opportunities

"Most people miss opportunities because it wears overalls and looks like work." Thomas Edison, a man who knew a thing or two about spotting opportunities.

Let's kick things off by sharpening our opportunity radar. Opportunities often lurk in the shadows of challenges, disguised as problems waiting to be solved. Look at the likes of Elon Musk, who turned the challenge of sustainable energy into the billion-dollar empire we know as Tesla. But it's not just about spotting opportunities; it's about knowing which ones align with your passion and skills. As Steve Jobs once quipped, "Your work is going to fill a large part of your life, and the only way to be truly satisfied is to do what you believe is great work." The exhilarating dance with opportunity—a waltz that requires a discerning eye, a dash of creativity, and a willingness to see beyond the obvious. As the illustrious Thomas Edison wittily noted, "Opportunity is missed by most people because it is dressed in overalls and looks like work." In these words, he encapsulated the essence of the entrepreneurial spirit, where hidden gems often masquerade as challenges.

In the year 2008 when the world was grappling with a financial crisis, amidst the chaos, Elon Musk, a maverick entrepreneur, sees not just adversity, but an opportunity cloaked in the guise of sustainability. The challenge of harnessing clean energy becomes his canvas and the result? The birth of Tesla, a billion-dollar empire, revolutionized the automotive industry.

Sharpening the Opportunity Radar

Our journey begins with the art of sharpening our opportunity radar, a skill that distinguishes visionaries from the ordinary. Opportunities, much like rare jewels, often hide in plain sight. They lurk in the shadows of challenges, waiting to be unearthed by those with the audacity to dream and the courage to act. Consider the iconic Steve Jobs, a maestro of innovation, his ability to see opportunities where others saw obstacles propelled Apple to unimaginable heights. The key lies not just in spotting opportunities but in aligning them with your passion and skills, the secret sauce that transforms work into a gratifying journey.

Elon Musk, a modern-day alchemist, possesses a unique ability to turn challenges into opportunities, transforming leaden obstacles into golden success. Take the case of Tesla, where Musk saw not just a need for sustainable energy but an opportunity to redefine an entire industry. In the realm of electric vehicles, he didn't just build cars; he engineered a revolution. Musk's journey illustrates that true entrepreneurs don't merely stumble upon opportunities, they create them. They understand that amidst the chaos of challenges, there lies a fertile ground for innovation and growth. It's a mindset that transforms problems into puzzles, with solutions waiting to be discovered.

Steve Jobs, the maestro of product design, recognized the symbiotic relationship between passion and skills. His statement, "Your work is going to fill a large part of your life, and the only way to be truly satisfied is to do what you believe is great work," is a manifesto for those seeking not just financial success but a profound sense of fulfillment. Identifying opportunities isn't a game of chance; it's a strategic dance where your passions and skills guide the steps. Jobs wasn't merely interested in creating products; he was on a quest to revolutionize industries. His work at Apple became an extension of his beliefs and a testament to the power of aligning professional pursuits with personal passion.

Musk's story teaches us that true entrepreneurial vision goes beyond financial gains; it's about leaving an indelible mark on the world. Aligning opportunities with a deeper purpose elevates the journey from mere profit-making to a meaningful endeavor that resonates with the values of the entrepreneur. In our exploration into the art of identifying opportunities, let Edison's words echo in your entrepreneurial soul: "Opportunity is missed by most people because it is dressed in overalls and looks like work." Seize the overalls, embrace the challenges, and dance with the opportunities that await in the realm of entrepreneurship. The stage is set, the music plays, and the overture of opportunity awaits your grand entrance.

Harnessing Creativity

Creativity is the heartbeat of entrepreneurship, the force that transforms mundane ideas into groundbreaking innovations. Ever wondered how a simple search engine became the tech behemoth we know as Google? Larry Page and Sergey Brin dared to dream big and embrace creativity. As Steve Jobs eloquently put it, "Innovation distinguishes between a leader and a follower." To unleash your entrepreneurial spirit, let your creativity run wild. Break free from the shackles of convention and ask yourself, "What if?" Remember, the first step to creating the next big thing is to imagine it.

In entrepreneurship, creativity stands as the undisputed maestro, orchestrating symphonies of innovation that reverberate through industries. It is the heartbeat, the life force that breathes vitality into the mundane, transforming ordinary ideas into groundbreaking innovations that shape the course of history. Consider the saga of Google, a company that sprouted from the fertile soil of creativity and blossomed into a tech behemoth that redefined the way we interact with information. Larry Page and Sergey Brin, the architects of Google, weren't content with the status quo. They dared to dream big, envisaging a world where information was not just accessible but organized and optimized. In pursing this vision, they unleashed their creative spirits, turning a simple search engine into a global powerhouse.

The Google Odyssey began with a simple yet audacious question: What if we could organize the world's information and make it universally accessible and useful? This question wasn't merely a spark; it was the ignition of a creative wildfire that burned through preconceived notions and forged a path to uncharted territories. The founders, Larry Page and Sergey Brin, exemplified the spirit of the entrepreneur as a creative visionary. They understood that to stand out in a crowded landscape, one must not only dream big but also embrace the transformative power of creativity. Innovation, as Steve Jobs so eloquently put it, distinguishes between a leader and a follower. In the realm of search engines, Google emerged not as a follower but as a pioneer, rewriting the rules and setting new standards for the digital age.

To unleash the full potential of your entrepreneurial spirit, it's imperative to liberate creativity from the confines of convention. Break free from the shackles that bind your ideas to the ordinary and let your imagination soar to unprecedented heights. Creativity flourishes in an environment that fosters unconventional thinking, where individuals question the norm and challenge the status quo. Consider the iconic

Steve Jobs, a trailblazer who embodied the ethnos of creative freedom. Throughout Apple's journey, he relentlessly pursued innovative ideas that transcended industry norms. From the Macintosh to the iPod, iPhone, and beyond, Job's ability to think differently was a testament to the transformative power of creative thinking.

At the heart of creativity lies the "What if" mindset—an invitation to explore the realm of possibility, challenge assumptions, and chart a course into unexplored territories. Asking "What if" is not just a query; it's a declaration of intent, a commitment to pushing the boundaries of what is known and venturing into the vast expanse of the unknown. A journey from the seed of an idea to a groundbreaking innovation often begins with this simple question: What if we could connect the world through a social network? Mark Zuckerberg posed this question, birthing Facebook and forever altering the landscape of digital communication. It's a testament to the transformative potential inherent in daring to ask, "What if?"

Imagination is the fertile soil in which the seeds of innovation germinate. To create the next big thing, one must conceive it in the realm of imagination. The power to visualize, to see beyond the constraints of the present, is the hallmark of a true creative entrepreneur. In the annals of technology, visionaries like Elon Musk exemplify turning imagination into reality. From envisioning a future where humanity is interplanetary to revolutionizing transportation with electric cars, Musk's imaginative prowess has propelled him into the pantheon of creative geniuses. His ventures, including SpaceX and Tesla, attest to the potency of imagination as the catalyst for transformative innovation.

As you navigate the landscape of entrepreneurship, remember that creativity is not a mere embellishment; it's the very essence of your journey. Channel your inner Larry Page, Sergey Brin, Steve Jobs, Mark Zuckerberg, and Elon Musk, unleash the creative storm within you, break free from convention, and let the "What if" mindset be your guiding star.

Cultivating the Mindset

A financial empire requires a fortress of resilience, and the cornerstone of that fortress is mindset. The entrepreneurial journey is not a stroll; it's a rollercoaster ride with twists, turns, and the occasional loop-de-loop. As the legendary Winston Churchill once said, "Success is not final, failure is not fatal: It is the courage to continue that counts." Embrace failure as a stepping stone to success. Let setbacks be the ink that colors the canvas of your experience. The entrepreneurial mindset thrives on adaptability, grit, and an insatiable hunger for improvement. So, fellow adventurers, as we set sail into the entrepreneurial seas, keep your eyes peeled for opportunities, let your creativity roam free, and fortify your mindset. This chapter is not just a guide; it's a compass pointing you toward the vast horizons of financial success. The journey has just begun, and the best is yet to come. So, tighten those entrepreneurial bootstraps and let the spirit within you soar!

In the world of entrepreneurship, failure isn't a sign of defeat; it's a rite of passage. As Winston Churchill once wisely remarked, "Success is stumbling from failure to failure with no loss of enthusiasm." Consider the tales of iconic entrepreneurs like Oprah Winfrey, who faced professional setbacks and rejection before ascending to media royalty. In its raw essence, failure is the crucible of growth that forges resilience and etches lessons into the very fabric of your journey. Think of failure not as a stop sign but as a yield, prompting you to reassess, recalibrate, and ultimately redirect your efforts. It's the entrepreneur's compass, pointing towards uncharted territories where success lies camouflaged in the guise of valuable lessons.

Imagine the journey of Jeff Bezos, the visionary behind Amazon, in the early days, setbacks and skepticism were his constant companions. Yet, each challenge was an opportunity to refine his strategy and vision. Setbacks are not roadblocks; they're merely pauses for recalibration. Think of setbacks as the ink that colors the canvas of your entrepreneurial experience. Each stroke is a lesson; each color is a nuanced understanding of the complex tapestry that is in the business world. The most compelling stories of success often emerge from the chapters marked by adversity.

The entrepreneurial path is not a straight line; it's a rollercoaster of unpredictable twists and turns. As Charles Darwin famously asserted, "It is not the strongest of the species that survive, nor the most intelligent, but the one most responsive to change." The ability to adapt is the secret weapon in an entrepreneur's arsenal. Consider the evolution of Nokia, once a titan in the mobile phone industry. Failure to adapt led to its decline, contrasting with companies like Apple, which embraced change and innovation. The business landscape is a dynamic terrain, and those who navigate it successfully do so with a keen eye on trends, a nimble approach to change, and an unwavering commitment to staying ahead of the curve.

Grit, that indomitable spirit to persevere in the face of adversity, is the true currency of entrepreneurship. As Angela Duckworth, the psychologist who popularized the concept of grit, asserts, "Grit is passion and perseverance for long-term goals." Consider the story of Colonel Sanders, who faced rejection 1009 times before finding a taker for his Kentucky Fried Chicken recipe. It was his grit that transformed him from a struggling retiree into a fast-food icon.

Grit isn't just about persistence; it's about maintaining passion and focus over the long haul. It's about weathering storms, conquering doubts, and emerging stronger on the other side. Grit and determination forge billionaires over time; they are not made overnight.

Insatiable Hunger for Improvement

Success isn't a destination; it's a journey marked by a perpetual thirst for improvement. The most successful entrepreneurs are perpetual learners, always seeking ways to enhance their skills, broaden their perspectives, and refine their strategies. Consider the late Steve Jobs, a relentless innovator who once remarked, "Stay hungry, stay foolish." The insatiable hunger for improvement propels entrepreneurs to transcend their current achievements and strive for greater heights. Whether it's through continuous education, embracing new technologies, or fostering a culture of innovation within your organization, the quest for improvement is the cornerstone of sustained success. So, my entrepreneurial compatriots, as you navigate the entrepreneurial rollercoaster, embrace failure as a guide, let setbacks be the vibrant hues on your canvas, and cultivate a mindset of adaptability, grit, and an insatiable hunger for improvement. The path to billions is not a smooth highway; it's a thrilling, unpredictable journey. Stay hungry, stay foolish, and let the entrepreneurial spirit within you flourish!

Chapter2

The Art of Risk-Taking

Thrill-seekers and future billionaires, welcome to the grand opening act of our financial adventure "The Art of Risk-Taking." Picture this chapter as a rollercoaster, a thrilling ride through calculated loops and daring plunges in the business world. Fasten your seatbelts, because in the pursuit of making a few billion dollars, mastering the art of risk-taking is not just a choice—it's the only way to ride.

Risk: The Entrepreneurial Palette

Let's begin by dipping our brushes into the colorful palette of risk. Quoting Vincent van Gogh's words, "I am seeking. I am striving. I am in it with all my heart." The business world is your canvas, and risk is the vibrant pigment that gives life to your masterpiece. But here's the kicker: it's not about wild strokes of chaos; it's about the strategic strokes that create a symphony of success.

Imagine Richard Branson, the maverick behind the Virgin Group. His journey is a canvas splashed with bold risk-taking. From launching Virgin Records with no industry experience in attempt global balloon flights, Branson's calculated risks have become the strokes of his success story. Remember, risk is not a leap into the abyss; it's a strategic dive into the pool of opportunity.

In this artistic endeavor, it's crucial to grasp that risk isn't about wild strokes of chaos, but strategic strokes that create a harmonious symphony. Imagine your canvas not as a chaotic jumble of colors but as a carefully orchestrated masterpiece, just as Van Gogh didn't haphazardly throw paint onto his canvas. Successful entrepreneurs don't take reckless gambles, they strategically choose their strokes, each one contributing to the grandeur of their entrepreneurial artwork.

Consider the audacious Richard Branson, the maverick behind the Virgin Group. His journey is a testament to the artistry of calculated risk-taking. Launching Virgin

Records with no industry experience? That's a bold stroke. Attempting global balloon flights? Another calculated risk that became a defining stroke in Branson's success story. Each move was a brushstroke on his canvas, creating a vibrant narrative of triumph over adversity.

Now, let's debunk the myth that risk is a leap into the abyss. No, dear entrepreneur, it's a strategic dive into the pool of opportunity. Imagine risk as a refreshing plunge, not a reckless jump without a safety net. This is where calculated decision-making comes into play, ensuring that each risk is well-measured and aligned with your broader vision. Consider the words of Sir Winston Churchill, who once said, "Success is not final, failure is not fatal: It is the courage to continue that counts." Courage, intertwined with strategic risk-taking, propels you forward. As Branson strategically dove into the uncharted territories of business, entrepreneurs can strategically navigate risks, transforming uncertainties into opportunities.

Now, some may argue, "But what if I make the wrong move? Won't I risk everything?" It's a valid consideration, and in the art of risk-taking, we don't dismiss caution. Instead, it's about understanding the canvas, knowing the potential outcomes, and making informed decisions. Risk is not about gambling your entire venture; it's about strategic choices that enhance your chances of success. As Mark Zuckerberg, the trailblazer behind Facebook, once remarked, "The biggest risk is not taking any risk. In a world that's changing really quickly, the only strategy that is guaranteed to fail is not taking risks." Zuckerberg's journey emphasizes the importance of calculated risks in a dynamic business landscape. Each calculated risk, each strategic stroke, contributes to the vibrant tapestry of your success. So, fellow artist of entrepreneurship, dip your brushes into the palette of risk, compose your symphony, and let the masterpiece of your financial dreams unfold on the canvas of opportunity. The entrepreneurial world awaits your strokes — paint boldly!

Strategic Decisions: Chess Moves in the Business Board

Now, let's play a game of chess in the business world. As chess grandmaster Garry Kasparov wisely noted, "You must take your opponent into a deep, dark forest where 2+2=5, and the path leading out, is only wide enough for one." Your strategic decisions serve as chess moves, and the market is the vast forest in this analogy. It's about anticipating your opponent's moves while paving a path to victory. Consider Jeff Bezos, the strategic chess master of e-commerce. When he introduced Amazon Prime, skeptics questioned the decision to offer free shipping. Yet, Bezos's strategic foresight saw beyond the immediate costs, paving the way for customer loyalty and unprecedented growth. Strategic decisions are not about playing safe; they're about playing smart in the business chessboard.

In this captivating game, strategic decisions are our chess moves—a series of calculated steps that require foresight and a touch of cunning. Imagine yourself as the grandmaster navigating through the dense market forest, where competitors lurk like hidden adversaries. The goal is not just to survive but to outmaneuver, outsmart, and emerge victorious. Jeff Bezos, the maestro of e-commerce, our strategic chess master, with his strategic foresight, envisioned a path beyond immediate costs. He saw it as a move to create customer loyalty, and oh, what a move it turned out to be! Amazon Prime became a game-changer, propelling Amazon to unprecedented growth.

Now, let's address the elephant in the room—the notion that strategic decisions are akin to playing it safe. Doubters may question, "Why not adhere to the familiar and proven methods?" Well, my savvy entrepreneurs, playing smart is not synonymous with playing safe. It's about understanding the dynamics of the business chessboard and making moves that position you for success. As the legendary boxer Muhammad Ali once said, "He who is not courageous enough to take risks will accomplish nothing in life." Think of strategic decisions as Ali's jabs and crosses in the ring — well-calculated, aimed at the opponent's vulnerabilities, and with a clear vision of victory. It's not about avoiding challenges; it's about navigating them with finesse.

Let's dive deeper into the strategic brilliance of Jeff Bezos, our chess master extraordinaire. When Amazon entered the e-commerce arena, it was a bold move in itself. But Bezos didn't stop there. He played the game strategically by introducing innovations like one-click purchasing, personalized recommendations, and the Kindle e-reader. These were not just moves; they were strategic gambits that disrupted the industry. Critics might have scoffed, competitors might have doubted, but Bezos, with his keen understanding of the chessboard, saw these moves as the key to reshaping the landscape of online retail. The result? Amazon became a global powerhouse, showcasing the power of strategic decisions in the business game.

Now, some skeptics might argue, "But what if my strategic move isn't convincing enough?" Well, my entrepreneurial comrades, the art lies not just in making moves but in convincing the audience—be it customers, stakeholders, or competitors—that your move is not just a move but a game-changer. Remember the skepticism when Apple eliminated the headphone jack from the iPhone? Critics questioned the move, doubting its practicality and potential backlash. However, Apple's strategic vision, led by Steve Jobs, saw a future where wireless audio would dominate. It was a move that not only proved convincing, but set a new standard in the smartphone industry.

As we wrap up this thrilling game of business chess, remember that strategic decisions are not just moves; they are the masterstrokes that lead to checkmate in the competitive landscape. So, entrepreneurs, channel your inner grandmaster, envision the market as your chessboard, and make strategic decisions that resonate with brilliance. The game is afoot, and victory awaits those who strategize, innovate, and make convincing moves in the grand theater of business. Onward to checkmate!

Calculated Risks

Now, let's talk about alchemy — the art of turning uncertainty into gold. As Warren Buffett sagely remarked, "Risk comes from not knowing what you're doing." Calculated risks are not blind gambles; they result from meticulous analysis and understanding. Think of Elon Musk, who invested his last $180 million in Tesla and SpaceX. Musk's calculated risks were not random bets; they were well-thought-out moves that paid off handsomely.

It's about acknowledging the potential pitfalls, weighing the odds, and making informed decisions. Calculated risks are the alchemical gold that transforms uncertainty into opportunity, propelling you closer to those coveted billion-dollar dreams. Alright, fellow risk-takers, buckle up for a thrilling journey into the alchemical realm of entrepreneurship—where uncertainty transforms into gold through the art of calculated risks. As the Oracle of Omaha, Warren Buffett sagely remarked, "Risk comes from not knowing what you're doing." So, let's unveil the secrets of turning uncertainty into opportunity, with a touch of inspiration from none other than Elon Musk.

Elon Musk, the modern-day alchemist of innovation, who invested his last $180 million into Tesla and SpaceX, not as a reckless gambler but as a calculated risk-taker. Musk's move wasn't a blind bet; it was a strategic decision crafted with precision and forethought. Here's a man who understands the alchemy of turning uncertainty into opportunity. Consider Tesla, an audacious venture that grew into an industry dominated by giants. Critics scoffed, but Musk, with his alchemical mindset, saw the potential for electric vehicles to redefine transportation. The calculated risk paid off handsomely, and Tesla is now synonymous with innovative innovation.

Now, let's address the skeptics who argue, "But what if things go south?" Well, fear not, my entrepreneurial comrades, for acknowledging potential pitfalls is the first step in the alchemical process. It's not about blind optimism; it's about a clear-eyed assessment of the landscape. As the wise Chinese military strategist Sun Tzu once said, "Know yourself, know your enemy, and you will win a hundred battles." In the business battlefield, knowing the potential pitfalls is equivalent to understanding your opponent. It's about being strategic, foreseeing challenges, and preparing for battle.

In the grand scheme of turning uncertainty into gold, weighing the odds is our entrepreneurial scale. It's about assessing the risks and rewards, and understanding that entrepreneurship is not a game of chance but a strategic endeavor. Elon Musk weighed the odds of investing in SpaceX, a private aerospace manufacturer. The space industry, a domain traditionally reserved for governments, seemed an unlikely venture. Yet, Musk's calculated risk was driven by a vision beyond Earth–the colonization of Mars by considering the odds, acknowledging the risks, and achieving a transformative result.

In the alchemical process of entrepreneurship, calculated risks are the mystical substance that propels you toward those coveted billion-dollar dreams. It's not a shortcut, but a strategic pathway that requires courage, analysis, and a touch of visionary magic. As J. K. Rowling, the sorceress of storytelling, once said, "It is impossible to live without failing at something unless you live so cautiously that you might as well not have lived at all." Calculated risks are the essence of truly living, of embracing the unknown with the anticipation of alchemical transformation. To explore the alchemy of calculated risks, remember that entrepreneurship is a grand symphony. Each calculated risk, when played with precision, contributes to the harmonious crescendo of success. So, fellow alchemists of opportunity venture forth with courage, acknowledge the potential pitfalls, and let the transformative magic of calculated risks turn uncertainty into the golden tapestry of your entrepreneurial dreams. Onward to the alchemical symphony of success!

Daring Ventures

Now, let's strap on our parachutes for daring ventures. Richard Branson once proclaimed, "The brave may not live forever, but the cautious do not live at all." Daring ventures are the bold strokes that carve new paths beyond the comfort zone. Take Oprah Winfrey, who ventured into launching her network, OWN. Critics questioned the move, citing the challenges and risks involved. Yet recklessness did not fuel Winfrey's audacity; it was a calculated leap into uncharted territory but her audacity led to a network that became a powerful force in media.

Daring ventures are not about recklessness; they are about calculated audacity. It's about stepping into the unknown, embracing uncertainty, and redefining the rules of the game. Those who dare may face challenges, but they also unlock doors to unparalleled opportunities.

Winfrey's journey into the unknown wasn't just about creating a network; it was about redefining the landscape of media. She faced challenges, but her audacious move led to the creation of OWN, a network that not only survived but thrived, becoming a powerful force in the media industry. This daring venture showcased that calculated audacity can turn skeptics into believers and redefine the rules of the game.

Daring ventures, far from being reckless endeavors, are the bold strokes that carve new paths beyond the comfort zone. They are the stories of individuals who embrace uncertainty with open arms, challenging the status quo and reshaping industries. It's not about blindly stepping into the abyss but about calculated audacity—a willingness to take risks for the sake of innovation.

Consider Elon Musk, the disruptor extraordinaire, venturing into electric vehicles and space exploration. He did not make his audacious move in ignorance of challenges; they were strategic decisions aimed at pushing the boundaries of what was possible. Musk's calculated audacity didn't just redefine industries; it propelled him into the ranks of visionary entrepreneurs who dared to dream big.

Now, skeptics might argue, "Isn't daring too risky? What about the potential pitfalls. Dear skeptics, ventures filled with daring aren't synonymous with recklessness. They involve a calculated assessment of risks, coupled with the audacity to challenge the norm. Daring entrepreneurs understand the potential challenges but view them as stepping stones, not roadblocks. As the wise Helen Keller once said, "Life is either a daring adventure or nothing at all." Daring ventures embody the spirit of adventure, where challenges are part of the journey, not deterrents. The audacious minds who venture beyond their comfort zones are the ones who leave an indelible mark on the canvas of innovation.

Remember that audacity is the key to unlocking unparalleled opportunities. It's about seeing challenges as invitations to innovate, and comfort zones as boundaries to be pushed. So, fellow adventurers, strap on your parachutes, embrace the uncertainty, and dive into the daring ventures that await on the horizon. The journey beyond the comfort zone is where audacious dreams transform into reality. Onward to unparalleled opportunities!

The Entrepreneurial Rollercoaster

Get ready for the highs and lows of the entrepreneurial rollercoaster, my friends. It's a ride where every twist and turn brings either exhilarating triumphs or heart-wrenching setbacks. As Rocky Balboa once said, "It's not about how hard you hit. It's about how hard you can get hit and keep moving." Consider the tale of J. K. Rowling, who faced rejection after rejection before the world embraced Harry Potter. The entrepreneurial journey was not a smooth ride; it was a rollercoaster with loops of success and drops of failure. But it's the ability to weather the lows and relish the highs that separates the thrill-seekers from the timid. Some skeptics might say, "But what about playing it safe? Isn't that the key to success?" Dear companions, choosing the safe path secures a cozy seat on the merry-go-round, but it won't thrust you onto the exhilarating rollercoaster of financial triumphs. The art of risk-taking isn't about being reckless; it's about being strategic, calculated, and bold.

Some might argue, "But what if I encounter failure?" Ah, failure is not the end; it's a pit stop on the road to success. Take a clue from Walt Disney, whose first animation company went bankrupt before he created the magical empire we know today. Failure is a fleeting deviation, not a permanent dead-end.

Imagine this rollercoaster as a pulsating heartbeat, racing with anticipation. Each loop of success sends adrenaline coursing through your veins, while every drop of failure feels like a sudden plunge into uncertainty. It's not a smooth ride; it's a thrilling symphony of highs and lows that defines the entrepreneurial spirit. Consider the saga of J. K. Rowling, a tale that resonates with every aspiring entrepreneur. Rowling, before the magical world of Harry Potter embraced her, faced rejection after rejection. Her manuscript encountered closed doors and skeptics who couldn't foresee the enchanting journey that awaited readers worldwide. Rowling's story is a testament to the rollercoaster, where the laws of rejection became the stepping stones to literary stardom.

It is possible to say, "Isn't the rollercoaster too uncertain? Why not opt for a smoother ride?" My courageous allies, the entrepreneurial journey is not for those without bravery. It's about weathering the lows with resilience and relishing the highs with unbridled joy. Just as a rollercoaster promises thrills, it also demands courage.

As Helen Keller once said, "Only through experience of trial and suffering can the soul be strengthened, ambition inspired, and success achieved." The entrepreneurial rollercoaster is where character is molded, ambitions are sparked, and success become a hard- earned victory.

Chapter3

Innovate or Stagnate

Welcome, to the vibrant realm of innovation – the beating heart of success in the dynamic landscape of wealth creation. In this exhilarating chapter, we embark on a journey through the corridors of groundbreaking ideas, where innovation isn't just a choice; it's the lifeline that propels individuals to the pinnacle of financial triumph. So, fasten your seatbelts as we explore those who dared to innovate and left an indelible mark on their industries.

Imagine innovation as a symphony, resonating through time, orchestrating progress with each transformative note. It's not merely a buzzword; it's the melody that harmonizes with the rhythms of success. As the illustrious Henry Ford once remarked, "If I had asked people what they wanted, they would have said faster horses." Ford's visionary leap into the unknown, the mass production of automobiles, wasn't just innovation;

it was a revolution that transformed transportation forever. Our symphony begins with the visionary crescendo of Henry Ford, an automotive maestro who dared to compose a melody beyond the expectations of his audience. In an era when horses still ruled the roads, Ford's audacious leap into the unknown – the mass production of automobiles – was more than just a note; it was a revolutionary movement that transformed the very fabric of transportation. The clatter of hooves is replaced by the rhythmic hum of engines, as Ford's assembly lines usher in an era where the horse-drawn carriage becomes a relic of the past. It wasn't merely a faster horse that people needed; it was a completely novel mode of transportation that Ford, with his visionary composition, delivered to the world. The automobile wasn't just a vehicle; it was a revolutionary refrain in the symphony of progress.

Innovation is not just a solitary note but a transformative melody that weaves through the fabric of time. It harmonizes with the rhythms of success, creating a harmonious interplay between creativity, vision, and societal needs. Innovation, as Ford demonstrated, isn't always about meeting existing demands; it's about anticipating unspoken desires and needs.

Consider the evolution of smartphones in our modern era. If Steve Jobs had merely asked people what they wanted, they might have envisioned a slightly upgraded mobile phone. However, Jobs, like Ford, orchestrated a transformative melody. The iPhone wasn't just an improvement; it was a revolutionary composition that merged communication, entertainment, and convenience into a single device.

It is possible to argue, "Isn't innovation risky? What if it disrupts rather than harmonizes?" Valid concerns, indeed. However, the symphony of progress, much like any masterpiece, requires harmony, dissonance, and the ability to navigate both. Ford's mass production faced sketicism and challenges, yet it harmonized with the changing needs of society. As Charles Kettering, another innovator, wisely noted, "The world hates change, yet it is the only thing that has brought progress." Ford's revolutionary leap wasn't without its dissonant chords, but it was precisely his willingness to harmonize with change that propelled transportation into a new era.

Let the echoes of innovation linger in the air. Innovation is not just a melody; it's a composition that transcends time, resonating with the spirit of progress. So, fellow innovators, play on! Embrace the dissonance, harmonize with change, and compose melodies that reverberate through the annals of history. Onward to a future where innovation is not just a note but a transformative symphony that shapes the rhythms of success!

Trailblazers of Innovation

Let's delve into the captivating case studies of trailblazing individuals who turned innovation into wealth creation. Consider the story of Steve Jobs, the maestro behind Apple. His audacious move to introduce the iPhone revolutionized not only the smartphone industry but altered the way we connect, communicate, and consume information. Jobs didn't just innovate; he orchestrated a technological symphony that echoed through the corridors of time.

Legendary Steve Jobs, the wizard of innovation who orchestrated a technological symphony that continues to reverberate through time. In a world where mobile phones were mere communication devices. Then, Jobs steps onto the stage with the iPhone, not just a phone but a revolutionary device that alters the very essence of how we connect, communicate, and consume information

Jobs wasn't content with incremental upgrades; he envisioned a device that blended elegance, functionality, and innovation. The iPhone wasn't merely a gadget; it was a cultural icon that transcended its utilitarian purpose. In Jobs' hands, innovation became a symphony

— each feature, each design element, harmonizing to create a masterpiece that disrupted industries and set new standards.

Jobs didn't just create a smartphone; he crafted an experience. He understood that innovation goes beyond the tangible; it's about the emotional resonance with users. The iPhone wasn't just a device; it was a manifestation of Jobs' vision to revolutionize how we interact with technology.

As we stroll down the memory lane of innovation, we encounter the indomitable Thomas Edison, the luminary whose inventions lit up the world. Edison's tale isn't just about a light bulb; it's a narrative of relentless pursuit and transformative power that echoes in every corner of our daily lives. Imagine a time when nights were shrouded in darkness, and Edison emerges with the invention that brightens not just rooms but the future of innovation. The light bulb wasn't merely a source of illumination; it became the catalyst for countless innovations that followed. Edison's pursuit wasn't confined to a single invention; it illuminated the path for others to follow, creating a cascade of progress. Skeptic might argue, "Wasn't Edison just lucky?" The truth is, Edison didn't achieve success by luck; it came from relentless experimentation, numerous failures, and a steadfast belief in the transformative potential of ideas. His legacy isn't just in the light bulb; it's in the mindset that innovation is a journey, not a destination.

As we conclude this innovators' tales, remember that innovation is a symphony – a harmonious interplay of creativity, vision, and the audacity to redefine norms. Jobs and Edison weren't just inventors; they were conductors of the innovation orchestra. So, fellow enthusiasts, let these stories inspire you to compose your own symphony of success. Onward to a future where innovation isn't just a concept; it's a vibrant melody that shapes the world!

Innovation as a Survival Strategy

In the ever-evolving business landscape, innovation isn't a luxury; it's a survival strategy. For instance, Kodak, once synonymous with photography, faced obsolescence as the digital era dawned. Entrenched in traditional film, the company faltered in innovating, resulting in the dwindling of its dominance. Consider the rise of Netflix, a disruptor that embraced streaming technology and redefined the entertainment industry. The juxtaposition is clear, innovate or face stagnation.

As Charles Darwin, the sage of evolution, accurately observed, "It is not the strongest of the species that survive, nor the most intelligent, but the one most responsive to change." The same principle applies in the business jungle; those who innovate, adapt, and evolve are the ones who thrive.

It is important to sail into the tumultuous sea of business evolution, where innovation isn't just a choice; it's a compass guiding us through uncharted waters. A once-mighty ship named Kodak, navigating the waves of the photography industry, faced obsolescence as the digital era dawned. Kodak found itself at a crossroads when digital photography emerged. The company, entrenched in the comforting familiarity of film, hesitated to embrace the winds of change. The result? The vessel, anchored in traditional film and its once unassailable dominance, dwindled like a ship lost in the fog. Kodak faced the harsh reality of obsolescence, a cautionary tale echoing through boardrooms as a stark reminder—innovation isn't a luxury; it's a necessity for survival.

It is possible to say, "Wasn't Kodak a powerhouse in its prime? Could it have survived the digital storm?" Innovation isn't about past glories; it's about the adaptability to future challenges. Kodak's reluctance to innovate wasn't a lack of resources or intelligence; it was a failure to recognize the shifting tides and adjust its course accordingly. The greater risk lies in stagnation. As the business jungle echoes with the sound of competition, those who refuse to innovate find themselves trapped in a time capsule while the world moves forward.

On the flip side of the innovation spectrum, let's spotlight the maverick rise of Netflix, a disruptor that embraced streaming technology and rewrote the rules of the entertainment industry. Imagine the landscape: traditional television ruled, and DVDs were the go-to for movie nights then, came Netflix with its innovative approach to content delivery–streaming.

While Kodak clung to its film reels, Netflix read the signs of change and embraced the digital tide. It wasn't just a shift in technology; it was a seismic transformation of how we consume entertainment. Netflix, with its adaptability and innovative mindset, not only survived but thrived in the ever-evolving digital era. The Kodak-Netflix dichotomy illustrates this principle vividly–those who resist change risk becoming relics, while the adaptive thrive in the business ecosystem.

In the world of innovation as a survival strategy, remember that in the business jungle, stagnation is the silent predator. Innovation is not just about keeping up; it's about forging ahead, anticipating shifts, and crafting your destiny in the ever-changing landscape. So, fellow navigators, let's hoist the sails of innovation, adapt to the winds of change, and chart a course to not just survive but thrive in the business seas ahead!

The Fear Factor

Imagine innovation as a thrilling adventure, a rollercoaster of possibilities. Yet, the fear of the unknown can cast a shadow on this excitement. It's true; innovation comes with risks. It's a bit like sailing into uncharted waters—exhilarating, yet uncertain. However, the true innovation dilemma lies not in the inherent risk but in succumbing to the fear that paralyzes us from taking that first step.

Let's draw inspiration from the cautionary tale of Blockbuster, once a giant in the video rental industry.

Picture the shelves lined with VHS tapes, the familiar blue and yellow logo signaling a movie night tradition. But, ah, here's where the plot thickens, Blockbuster hesitated at the precipice of the digital age, reluctant to adapt, and lay the seeds of its demise.

Blockbuster's reluctance to embrace the winds of digital change allowed nimble innovators like Netflix to swoop in and seize the opportunity. The demise of Blockbuster wasn't a result of innovation itself; it was the consequence of a glaring lack thereof. The lesson here is crystal clear: it's not the innovation that failed; it's failing to innovate.

The skeptics might interject, "But isn't stability safer than innovation? What if it leads to a misstep?" A fair point, but let's look at it this way—standing still in the ever-changing landscape of business is like trying to avoid waves in the ocean; eventually, the tide catches up. Innovation is the life jacket that helps businesses ride the waves rather than being engulfed by them.

As Steve Jobs wisely noted, "Innovation distinguishes between a leader and a follower." It's not about blindly chasing every trend but cultivating an innovation mindset — an openness to change, a willingness to adapt, and a belief in the transformative power of ideas. So, dear skeptics, let's reframe the narrative. Innovation isn't a leap into the abyss; it's a strategic dance with change. The real risk is not in the daring moves, but in the hesitation that leaves businesses stranded on the shores of stagnation. Embrace the innovation dilemma as a challenge to overcome, not a pitfall to avoid. Onward to a future where innovation isn't a risk but a thrilling journey towards progress!

Innovation is not just a choice, it is imperative to pursue financial success. Innovation is the compass that guides the entrepreneurial ship through uncharted waters, ensuring it doesn't merely survive but thrives in the vast sea of opportunities.

Chapter4

Financial Mastery

Welcome, dear readers, to the beating heart of financial prowess "Financial Mastery." In this exhilarating leg of our journey through the labyrinth of wealth creation, we will unravel the secrets, strategies, and mindset of those who have not only accumulated immense wealth but have mastered the delicate art of preserving it with finesse. So fasten your seatbelts as we embark on a voyage through the intricate world of finance.

Navigating the Chessboard of Investments

Imagine the financial world as a grand chessboard, where every move counts and strategic thinking reigns supreme. In this section, we'll dive into the diverse investment strategies that financial titans employ to navigate this intricate board. Take a page from the playbook of Warren Buffett, the Oracle of Omaha, who transformed the stock market into his canvas, strategically placing each piece to build an empire. From high-risk ventures to calculated investments, we'll explore the multifaceted moves that shape the financial destinies of the elite. "In the realm of finance, success hinges not on making moves but on making the correct moves."

Just as a chess grandmaster calculates each move, financial titans approach their investments with strategic thinking that reigns supreme. Imagine Warren Buffett as our chess grandmaster, the Oracle of Omaha, whose moves on the stock market canvas have painted a masterpiece of wealth creation. His playbook is a testament to the art of strategically placing each investment piece to build an empire.

Consider high-risk ventures as daring gambits, where the financial titans willingly sacrifice a pawn for the potential of a game-changing move. Calculated investments are like meticulous positioning of powerful pieces, anticipating the opponent's moves, and creating a foundation for long-term success.

In the financial chessboard, Warren Buffett's masterstroke is the creation of the Berkshire Hathaway Empire. Each acquisition, each investment, is a move carefully calculated to capture value and strengthen the overall position. Take the acquisition of companies like Coca-Cola or the strategic investments in Apple — each move strategically aligns to build and preserve wealth. "In financial chess, the true genius lies not in making complex moves but in making simple moves with profound impact." Some might object, "Isn't this chessboard filled with risks? What if a move backfires?" Undoubtedly, these concerns are reasonable, but the grace of strategic thinking becomes clear in this context. Acknowledging risk, but taking calculated risks. Just as in chess, not every move guarantees victory, but a thoughtful strategy minimizes the potential pitfalls. Every financial chess player knows that the game involves uncertainties, and they approach it with a blend of confidence, risk assessment, and adaptability.

In this financial chessboard, moves are not monotonous; they form a symphony. From the initial moves of pawns (smaller investments) to the strategic positioning of knights and bishops (diverse assets), leading to the powerful moves of rooks (major acquisitions) and the final checkmate with the king (ultimate financial success), orchestrating the journey with precision. "Creating financial success involves more than grand gestures; it requires the orchestration of well-considered moves that culminate in a symphony of wealth generation."

In the chessboard of investments, remember that each investor has their own unique game. It's not about replicating someone else's moves but understanding the principles of strategic thinking. Like a chess player, anticipate the moves, adapt to the changing board, and play your own game. The financial chessboard is vast, but with the right moves, you too can build your empire and declare checkmate on financial success. Onward to the next move in your own financial game!

Preserving Wealth: The Art and Science

Wealth preservation is not a passive act; it's an art and a science. "Safeguarding wealth is akin to nurturing a fragile garden, demanding perpetual care, attention, and a deep comprehension of the surroundings." Trust structures, tax optimization, and other sophisticated are important tools used by financial maestros to ensure their billions withstand the tests of time. Tales will unfold among those who not only made billions but mastered the subtle dance between risk and preservation.

Imagine preserving wealth as tending to a delicate garden—a lush expanse of financial assets, each requiring nurturing and protection. This metaphor illustrates the essence of wealth preservation: the need for constant vigilance, understanding the unique needs of each financial "plant," and adapting to the ever-changing economic climate. "Preserving wealth is not just about planting seeds; it's about cultivating a thriving garden that endures seasons and bears fruit for generations to come." In this financial garden, financial maestros employ sophisticated tools as their trusted aides. Trust structures, akin to the sturdy trellises supporting the vines, provide a framework for stability and protection. Tax optimization acts as the sunlight, ensuring that the wealth garden flourishes without being overshadowed by unnecessary tax burdens. These tools, when wielded with precision, create a resilient environment where wealth can not only survive but thrive.

Wealth preservation is not about burying assets in a financial bunker; it's a dance between risk and preservation. Consider the tale of a tightrope walker in the financial circus, balancing between the allure of high-risk ventures and the security of conservative investments. Financial maestros, akin to skilled dancers, skillfully take bold steps and gracefully retreat, creating a symphony of financial moves that harmonize risk and preservation. "In the ballet of wealth preservation, each move is deliberate, calculated, and contributes to the timeless masterpiece of financial stability."

In the exploration of the delicate art and science of wealth preservation, remember that preserving wealth is a journey, not a destination. It's about nurturing the seeds of prosperity, understanding the nuances of the financial ecosystem, and dancing to the rhythm of economic changes. So, fellow gardeners of wealth, let's tend to our financial landscapes with care, cultivate resilience, and ensure that our wealth gardens bloom with abundance for generations to come. Onward to a future where financial prosperity is not just accumulated but preserved as a timeless legacy!

The Mindset of Financial Titans

Beyond the numbers and strategies lies a mindset that sets financial titans apart. In this section, we'll delve into the minds of those who've not just conquered the intricacies of finance but have molded a mindset that attracts and multiplies wealth. Learn how successful individuals view risk, seize opportunities, and cultivate the resilience necessary to weather financial storms. "Riches involve more than just numerical values; it's a mindset that draws in prosperity."

Spotting Hidden Opportunities

The financial world is a treasure trove of hidden opportunities, waiting to be discovered by those with a discerning eye. We will unveil the secrets of spotting opportunities in unexpected places—from emerging markets to unconventional investment vehicles. Through tales of visionaries who turned unconventional opportunities into golden assets, you'll gain insights into how to transform the ordinary into the extraordinary.

"In the vast ocean of finance, hidden treasures await those with the courage to dive into the depths of the unknown."

Imagine the financial world as a treasure map, with emerging markets as the unexplored territories brimming with potential riches. These markets, often overlooked or underestimated, hold hidden treasures for those willing to venture beyond the familiar. Consider the tale of an adventurous entrepreneur who, recognizing the potential of a burgeoning economy, invested early and reaped rewards as the market blossomed. "In the treasure hunt of finance, emerging markets are the X marks on the spot, waiting to reveal their hidden riches to intrepid explorers."

Our financial odyssey doesn't stop at traditional shores; it ventures into the realm of unconventional investment vehicles. Think of these as uncharted islands that, when explored wisely, can yield treasures beyond imagination. Explore the story of a maverick investor who, instead of following the herd, sought opportunities in unconventional assets like rare collectibles or renewable energy startups, turning the ordinary rules of investment on their head.

As we navigate the financial odyssey, a recurring theme emerges—the courage to dive into the depths of the unknown. Just as a fearless explorer braves uncharted waters to discover new lands, the successful investor must muster the courage to explore uncharted financial territories. In the vast ocean of finance, hidden treasures await those with the audacity to venture into the unknown, armed with curiosity, foresight, and a willingness to take calculated risks.

However, our financial odyssey reminds us that every treasure comes with its challenges. While the seas may be choppy, success often lies in navigating the waves with skill and resilience. Just as a skilled sailor learns to read the signs of the ocean, a savvy investor learns to discern the nuances of the financial landscape. The greatest opportunities often lie beyond the horizon of the familiar. The financial odyssey is a journey of discovery, courage, and the willingness to see potential where others see only uncertainty. So, fellow adventurers of finance set sail into the unknown, where hidden treasures await those with the audacity to embrace the thrill of the undiscovered. Onward to a future where the ordinary transforms into the extraordinary, and the financial odyssey becomes a legendary tale of success!

Navigating Economic Shifts

The world of finance is dynamic, shaped by economic shifts and global events. This section equips you with the tools to not just react but proactively navigate these shifts. Explore the strategies employed by financial wizards during economic downturns and upswings on how they turned volatility into opportunities for unparalleled growth and how adaptation, not resistance, leads to financial mastery. "In the dance of economic shifts, those who lead the steps find themselves at the center of the ballroom." Here, you won't just learn to react; you'll master the art of proactive navigation through the twists and turns of financial choreography. Imagine economic downturns as an unexpected dips in the financial dance, rather than stumbling, financial wizards embrace these moments, executing moves that turn crisis into opportunity.

Explore the tale of a savvy investor who, during a recession, strategically invested in undervalued assets, later witnessing substantial returns when the market rebounded. This illustrates that downturns aren't the end of the dance; they're a chance for a graceful pivot. "In the realm of financial ballet, economic downturns aren't the conclusion; rather, they offer a chance for a splendid whirl toward loftier summits".

As economic upswings sweep through the ballroom, financial wizards don't just follow the rhythm; they lead the dance. Picture the entrepreneur who, recognizing an upswing, boldly expanded their business empire, leveraging the wave of prosperity. Through their stories, you'll grasp the importance of not merely riding the waves but orchestrating the dance, ensuring that each step aligns with the broader rhythm of economic growth. "In the symphony of finance, economic upswings are the crescendos and financial wizards are the conductors, orchestrating success with each well-timed move."

Financial mastery doesn't come from resisting change; it stems from skillfully adapting to economic shifts. Consider the analogy of a dance partner who seamlessly adjusts their steps to the changing tempo. Financial wizards, too, adapt their strategies, making timely adjustments that align with the evolving financial landscape.

Volatility in the financial dance isn't a disruption; it's a showcase of resilience. Explore the stories of investors who, rather than fearing market fluctuations, embraced them; how they strategically diversified their portfolios to mitigate risks, transforming the unpredictable into a choreographed display of financial strength. These examples serve as a testament that volatility, when embraced, can be a stepping stone to financial excellence. "In the financial dance, volatility serves as the beat that distinguishes remarkable dancers from the cautious wallflowers." Skeptics may express reservations about the prudence of embracing economic shifts because of the uncertainty they bring. They may also question the wisdom of embracing economic shifts, fearing the unknown. Yet, the dance of finance reminds us that every rhythm, even if unfamiliar, offers an opportunity for expression. Successful financial dancers comprehend that knowledge, preparation, and a willingness to embrace the unpredictable tempo of the financial dance floor conquer the fear of the unknown.

In the dance of economic shifts, remember that financial mastery is about leading the steps, not just following them. The financial dance is dynamic, and those who confidently navigate the ballroom find themselves at the center, orchestrating success with each move. Accumulating and preserving billions is not just about financial wizardry; it's about mastering the art of orchestrating wealth with precision and finesse. So, fellow dancers of finance, let's embrace the rhythm of economic shifts, adapting our steps to the ever-changing beats, and lead the dance towards unparalleled financial mastery. Onward to a future where economic shifts become opportunities, and the financial dance is a testament to your skillful navigation!

Chapter 5

Building a Powerful Network

Welcome to the world of interconnected success, where the strength of your network can be the key to unlocking unprecedented opportunities. In this chapter, we'll delve into the importance of connections and relationships in the business realm, unveiling strategies that go beyond handshakes to cultivate meaningful partnerships. Get ready to discover how leveraging your network can propel you toward the coveted realm of billionaires.

The Power of Connections: More than Just Handshakes

Picture your network as a vast tapestry woven with threads of connections that can shape your business destiny. It's not just about the number of business cards you collect; it's about forging genuine connections that withstand the test of time. Consider the journey of a budding entrepreneur who, through networking events, not only expanded their contact list but found mentors, collaborators, and lifelong friends, creating a support system that propelled their success. "In the intricate dance of business, connections are the music that harmonizes your journey, turning a solo performance into a symphony of shared success."

In the grand ballroom of business, imagine your network as a magnificent tapestry, each thread representing a connection that weaves the story of your entrepreneurial journey. It transcends the mere exchange of business cards; it's about cultivating genuine connections that stand resilient against the tests of time. Let me illustrate this concept with the tale of Alex, a budding entrepreneur who transformed a simple contact list into a tapestry of triumph.

Alex, armed with ambition and a handful of business cards, ventured into networking events not as a solo performer but as part of the intricate dance of business. Unlike those fixated on quantity, Alex focused on the quality of connections, understanding that forging authentic relationships was the key to unlocking the symphony of shared success. "In the bustling dance of business, every connection is a note in the symphony of your journey, creating a harmony that resonates with shared triumphs." Consider the mentorship Alex found in a seasoned industry expert he met at a conference. This mentor not only provided valuable insights but also became a guiding force, steering Alex away from pitfalls and towards opportunities. The mentorship wasn't a transactional exchange but a genuine connection, a thread woven into the fabric of Alex's success. Collaboration also played a pivotal role in Alex's narrative. A chance meeting at a networking luncheon led to a partnership with a like-minded entrepreneur, amplifying both of their strengths. What began as a casual conversation flourished into a strategic alliance, demonstrating that success weaves a richer tapestry when collaborative threads intertwine with kindled spirit. Lifelong friends emerged from the shared experiences of navigating the business landscape. These friendships weren't just for socializing; they became pillars of support, offering encouragement during challenging times and celebrating victories together. "In the journey of business, shared success with friends transforms the solo performance into a harmonious symphony."

Some might argue that networking is inherently transactional, a superficial exchange of business cards with no lasting impact. However, Alex's story refutes this notion, illustrating that networking is not about quantity but quality. It's about finding mentors who genuinely invest in your success, collaborators who amplify your strengths, and friends who stand by you on the entrepreneurial journey. In the tapestry of business connections, remember that your network is more than a collection of contacts; it's your tale of triumph. The quantity of threads composes the symphony of shared success not by their quality. So, fellow entrepreneurs, let's continue weaving our tapestries, recognizing that every connection, mentorship, collaboration, and friendship contributes to the harmonious symphony that propels us toward unparalleled success. Onward to a future where the intricate dance of business becomes a celebration of shared victories!

Strategies for Effective Networking

Effective networking is an art form, requiring more than just small talk and superficial exchanges. Explore the strategies employed by successful networkers, such as active listening, genuine curiosity, and the ability to add value to every interaction. Let's explore how a well-crafted conversation at a networking event can blossom into a transformative partnership, showcasing that the depth of your connections matters more than the breadth. "In the grand gallery of networking, every meaningful conversation is a stroke that adds color to the masterpiece of your business journey."

In the dynamic realm of business, effective networking is not a mere exchange of pleasantries; it's an art form that requires finesse, genuine engagement, and the ability to transform conversations into meaningful connections. Let's uncover the strategies employed by successful networkers, exploring the nuances that turn casual interactions into transformative partnerships, illustrated through real-world examples that paint a vivid picture of networking mastery.

Consider the story of Maya, a skilled networker who understands that effective communication is a two-way street. Maya doesn't just talk; she listens actively. At networking events, Maya engages in conversations with genuine curiosity, seeking to understand the needs, aspirations, and challenges of those she interacts with. Through this attentive listening, Maya doesn't just collect contacts; she cultivates connections, discovering common ground that becomes the foundation for future collaborations. "In the symphony of networking, active listening is the silent conductor that orchestrates harmony, transforming conversations into lasting connections."

Meet James, a primary networker known for his genuine curiosity. Instead of reciting rehearsed elevator pitches, James sparks conversations by asking insightful questions. He doesn't just inquire about business; he delves into personal stories, passions, and the journeys of fellow networkers. By expressing genuine interest, James transforms every interaction into a discovery process, uncovering opportunities and building relationships that extend beyond the confines of the event. "In the canvas of networking, genuine curiosity is the brushstroke that adds depth and dimension, revealing hidden opportunities beneath the surface.

Now, let's journey with Sarah, who understands that networking is not a one-sided exchange, but a reciprocal process. Sarah strives to add value to every interaction. Whether it's sharing insights, providing resources, or connecting individuals with mutual benefits, Sarah contributes to the success of others. This commitment to adding value makes her a sought-after networker, as her connections recognize every encounter as an opportunity for mutual growth. "In the mosaic of networking, adding value is the vibrant tile that enhances the overall picture, creating a masterpiece of interconnected success."

Now, let's journey with Sarah, who understands that networking is not a one-sided exchange, but a reciprocal process.

In the grand gallery of networking, depth matters more than breadth. Consider Alex, who, instead of collecting an extensive list of contacts, focuses on building meaningful connections. Alex invests time in cultivating relationships, turning acquaintances into allies. The result is a network that not only opens doors to opportunities but becomes a tight-knit community where support, collaboration, and shared successes flourish. "Every meaningful conversation is a stroke that adds color to the masterpiece of your business journey. Depth in connections transforms the gallery of your network into a vibrant tapestry of shared triumphs."

It is possible to say that networking is inherently superficial, revolving around polished pitches and surface-level interactions. However, the stories of Maya, James, Sarah, and Alex show that effective networking is about depth, authenticity, and a genuine commitment to building lasting connections.

In the exploration of networking mastery, remember that every meaningful conversation is a stroke that adds color to the masterpiece of your business journey. In the grand gallery of networking, depth, active listening, genuine curiosity, and the value you add to every connection, create a canvas where your entrepreneurial story unfolds with vibrancy and shared success. Onward to a future where the art of networking becomes a celebration of interconnected triumphs!

Cultivating Meaningful Partnerships

The true power of networking lies in transforming acquaintances into allies, collaborators, and partners. Journey with a seasoned entrepreneur who, through cultivating meaningful relationships, built a network of trusted partners. These partnerships became the cornerstone of joint ventures, shared successes, and an exponential amplification of opportunities. It's not just about knowing people; it's about knowing the right people and forging alliances that elevate both parties. "In the ecosystem of business, meaningful partnerships are the symbiotic relationships that fuel growth, with each party contributing to the success of the other."

Your network is not a static list, but a dynamic force that can catalyze your success. "In the realm of business, your network is not just a safety net; it's a catapult that propels you to heights you might not reach on your own." Let's delve into the strategic prowess of successful individuals who transform their networks into catalysts for achievement, illustrating through examples how a well-nurtured network becomes a formidable resource on the journey to the billion-dollar echelon.

Meet Emily, a visionary entrepreneur who understands that a network isn't just about who you know but how strategically you leverage those connections. When Emily embarked on a new venture, she strategically tapped into her network for resources, guidance, and opportunities. Instead of seeing her contacts as static entries in a directory, Emily transformed them into dynamic catalysts for her success. "In the symphony of business, your network is not just the audience; it's the orchestra that plays the notes of opportunity, turning your business venture into a harmonious success story."

Consider the narrative of John, who, in the pursuit of turning his innovative idea into reality, strategically used his network to secure investments. Instead of relying solely on traditional funding avenues, John turned to his network for potential investors. The relationships he had cultivated over time became the pillars of financial support, turning his entrepreneurial dreams into a well-funded reality. "Your network is more than a safety net; it's a financial arsenal providing the resources to propel you into the stratosphere of success."

Now, let's explore the journey of Sarah, an aspiring tech entrepreneur. Recognizing the gaps in her expertise, Sarah strategically reached out to her network for guidance. Through well-nurtured connections, Sarah gained access to niche expertise, mentorship, and industry insights that proved invaluable in navigating the complexities of her chosen field. Her network wasn't just a static list; it was a treasury of knowledge waiting to be unlocked. "In the dynamic rhythm of business, your network is more than a mere collection of names; it serves as a reservoir of expertise, a treasure trove that individuals can access to overcome challenges and seize opportunities."

Meet Alex, an introverted entrepreneur whose quiet demeanor defies the extroverted stereotype often associated with networking. Alex's story illustrates that effective networking isn't about flashy self-promotion but the art of building authentic connections. In a world where authenticity reigns supreme, Alex discovered that being genuinely interested in others and fostering meaningful relationships became the cornerstone of his networking success. "Networking is not a performance; it's a conversation. It's about creating genuine connections that go beyond the superficial layers, weaving a tapestry of relationships rooted in authenticity." Consider the journey of Maya, a savvy business professional who realized that effective networking goes beyond the exchange of business cards. Maya's story is a testament to the power of adding value to every interaction. By offering insights, sharing resources, and providing support to her network, Maya transformed networking from a transactional affair into a reciprocal exchange of value. "In the dynamic choreography of networking, value serves as the currency that propels relationships forward. The more you give, the richer your network becomes."

It is possible to argue that networking is a one-size-fits-all endeavor, but the reality is quite the opposite. Enter the world of diverse networking styles, where individuals like Chris, known for their unconventional approaches, challenge the notion of conformity. Chris showcases that effective networking is about finding your unique style, whether it involves attending traditional events or forging connections through innovative digital platforms. "Networking is a personalized journey. It's about discovering your unique style, embracing diversity, and creating a network that resonates with your goals and personality." Some might argue that strategic networking is opportunistic and self-serving. However, Emily, John, and Sarah's stories debunk this myth by showcasing that strategic networking is about reciprocity. It's not just about taking; it's about cultivating genuine relationships that evolve into mutually beneficial partnerships. Also, it is possible to argue that networking is solely about self-promotion or that it only benefits those with an extroverted nature. However, the stories within this chapter dispel these myths, illustrating that effective networking is about building authentic connections, adding value, and being genuinely interested in the success of others.

Your network is not just a safety net; it's a catapult propelling you into heights unimagined. The stories of Emily, John, and Sarah echo the sentiment that a well-nurtured, strategically leveraged network is a force that transforms business endeavors into resounding successes.

However, stories like Alex's, Maya's, and Chris's dismantle this myth that effective networking is something only extroverts can excel at, highlighting that introverts and extroverts alike can excel in the art of building connections. Networking is not about one's ability to work a room but the ability to forge meaningful relationships, regardless of personality traits. As we demystify the misconceptions surrounding networking, remember that it's not a stage for self-promotion but a harmonious symphony where authentic connections, value addition, and diverse styles converge. Alex, Maya, and Chris's stories echo the sentiment that effective networking is a dynamic, personalized journey, accessible to all who will embrace its true essence. So, let's tune into the melody of networking and compose our unique and authentic chapters within the grand symphony of business relationships!

Onward to a future where our networks are not just collections of contacts but dynamic catalysts in the symphony of our entrepreneurial journeys! Remember that your network is not just a collection of names; it's your net worth. The art of networking goes beyond transactions; it's about building relationships that endure and thrive. So, fellow networkers, let's weave the tapestry of success through genuine connections, strategic partnerships, and the shared triumphs of a network that propels us toward the coveted realm of making a few billion dollars. Onward to a future where every handshake, conversation, and partnership becomes a stepping stone toward unparalleled success!

Chapter 6

Strategic Negotiations

In the intricate dance of business, negotiation emerges as the skill that can transform discussions into stepping stones toward billion-dollar success. Picture the negotiating table as the battlefield, where strategic maneuvers and tactical brilliance can secure lucrative deals and helpful partnerships. In this chapter, we unravel the art of strategic negotiations, delving into proven techniques and learning from seasoned negotiators who have elevated every conversation into a pathway leading to unprecedented wealth.

The Symphony of Negotiation

Imagine negotiation as a symphony, each conversation a note contributing to the harmonious melody of business success. Legendary negotiator Robert Shapiro once said, "Negotiation is not about winning or losing; it's crafting an agreement that propels both parties toward their goals." This sets the stage for our exploration, emphasizing that negotiations aren't battles but collaborations, where both parties can orchestrate a symphony of success. Picture the negotiating table as a grand stage, and negotiation as a symphony, where each conversation contributes to the harmonious melody of business success. The analogy draws inspiration from the insightful words of legendary negotiator Robert Shapiro, who highlighted that negotiation transcends the simplistic notions of winning or losing. As we embark on this exploration, let's uncover the nuances of negotiation, showcasing that it is more of a collaborative symphony than a contentious battle. "Negotiation is not about winning or losing; it's crafting an agreement that propels both parties toward their goals." - Robert Shapiro

In the negotiation symphony, the conventional dichotomy of winners and losers dissolves, making room for a more nuanced perspective. Consider the historical Camp David Accords between Egypt and Israel. Anwar

Sadat, Menachem Begin, and mediator Jimmy Carter didn't fixate on winning or losing; instead, they orchestrated a historic agreement that reshaped regional dynamics. "Negotiation is a collaborative composition, where both parties contribute to the creation of a mutually beneficial arrangement." Delve into the Cuban Missile Crisis, a pivotal moment during the Cold War. President John F. Kennedy's negotiations with Soviet Premier Nikita Khrushchev exemplify the complexity of international negotiations. The avoidance of nuclear conflict showcased the power of crafting agreements that serve the greater good, emphasizing collaboration over confrontational strategies. "In the negotiation symphony, even amidst intense conflict, thoughtful and strategic agreements can achieve harmony." Explore the collaboration between Microsoft and IBM, where negotiations led to the creation of the first personal computer. Bill Gates and Microsoft negotiated a deal that allowed them to create an operating system for IBM's PC. This collaboration not only propelled both companies to unparalleled success but also played a pivotal role in the technological revolution. "Negotiation is not just about the terms of a deal; it's about crafting collaborations that can reshape industries and drive innovation."

In the negotiation symphony, success lies not in overpowering the other party, but in creating a harmonious arrangement that resonates with both. This approach addresses potential objections that negotiations are zero-sum games and instead promotes the idea that successful negotiations can lead to outcomes where everyone wins. Embrace the collaborative spirit, understand the power of crafting agreements that propel both parties forward, and recognize that every conversation is a note in the symphony of your business success. Negotiation, when approached with the mindset of collaboration, can indeed be a delightful and harmonious process, paving the way for unprecedented achievements in the world of business.

Mastering the Chessboard of Negotiation Strategies

Step onto the chessboard of negotiation strategies, where every move can alter the course of the game. Take a cue from the strategic brilliance of diplomats like Henry Kissinger, who turned delicate negotiations into global triumphs. Whether it's building rapport, understanding the opponent's motivations, or strategically revealing your cards, we'll explore the multifaceted strategies that transform negotiators into maestros. "In negotiation, it's not about outplaying your opponent; it's about creating a win-win scenario where both parties leave the table with a sense of accomplishment." Imagine negotiation as a captivating chess match, each move holding the potential to reshape the course of the game. Stepping onto this strategic chessboard, we draw inspiration from the diplomatic brilliance of figures like Henry Kissinger.

Whether it's the art of building rapport, deciphering the motivations of your counterpart, or strategically revealing your cards, let's embark on a journey to explore the multifaceted strategies that elevate negotiators to the status of maestros.

Henry Kissinger is a diplomat renowned for navigating complex international relations. In the negotiations leading to the Camp David Accords, Kissinger showcased the power of strategic brilliance. By understanding the underlying motivations of the parties involved, he orchestrated an agreement that reshaped the Middle East. This exemplifies the idea that negotiation is not just a series of moves, but a strategic dance where understanding your opponent is key. "In the chessboard of negotiation, understanding your counterpart's motivations is akin to expecting their next move, allowing you to navigate the game strategically." Explore the importance of building rapport in negotiations, a strategy often underestimated. Take a leaf from the book of successful negotiators who recognize that establishing a connection goes beyond the terms of the deal. Consider a scenario where a simple act of finding common ground or sharing a laugh during negotiations transforms the atmosphere, creating a collaborative space where both parties feel comfortable. "Building rapport is not just a nicety; it's a strategic move that lays the foundation for trust, collaboration, and a positive negotiation environment."

In the chessboard of negotiation, understanding the motivations behind each move is pivotal. Analyze real-world examples where negotiators, instead of solely focusing on the visible aspects of the deal, delved deeper into the motivations driving their counterparts. This approach allowed them to tailor their strategies, ensuring that the negotiated outcomes align with the true intentions of all parties involved. "Decoding motivations is like deciphering the chessboard; it gives you the insights needed to make strategic moves that align with the overall objectives of both parties."

Master the skill of strategically revealing your cards when negotiating. The chessboard analogy extends here, emphasizing that revealing certain pieces of your strategy strategically can lead to a more cooperative and collaborative atmosphere. "Strategic revelation is not a vulnerability; it's a calculated move that fosters trust and transparency, creating a conducive environment for mutually beneficial agreements."

In the grand symphony of negotiation, the ultimate goal is not to outplay your opponent but to create a win-win scenario. Let us analyze how negotiators, by focusing on collaborative outcomes, leave the table with a sense of accomplishment. This strategy challenges the notion that negotiation is a zero-sum game, emphasizing that success is not measured by the defeat of the other party but by the creation of shared victories. "In negotiation, the true triumph lies in crafting agreements that leave both parties feeling fulfilled, setting the stage for lasting partnerships and future collaborations." As we navigate the chessboard of negotiation strategies, remember that each move contributes to the evolving symphony of business diplomacy. By adopting a strategic mindset, understanding motivations, and fostering collaboration, negotiators can transform the game into a harmonious dance where success is measured by the collective achievements of all parties involved.

The Art of Silence: A Powerful Negotiation Tool

Silence isn't merely the absence of words; it's a potent tool in the arsenal of a skilled negotiator. Learn from the likes of Warren Buffett, who uses silence to his advantage during negotiations. We'll unravel the art of leveraging silence – how it can prompt concessions, create discomfort, and lead to favorable outcomes. Silence isn't just golden; it's a currency that can be exchanged for strategic advantage. "In negotiations, silence isn't emptiness; it's the pregnant pause that births favorable outcomes."

Silence isn't merely the absence of words; it's a potent tool in the arsenal of a skilled negotiator. Learn from the likes of Warren Buffett, who uses silence to his advantage during negotiations. We'll unravel the art of leveraging silence — how it can prompt concessions, create discomfort, and lead to favorable outcomes. Silence isn't just golden; it's a currency that can be exchanged for strategic advantage. "In negotiations, silence isn't emptiness; it's the pregnant pause that births favorable outcomes.

Warren Buffett is considered the sage of investment and has mastered the art of strategic silence. Buffett, known for his calm and composed demeanor, strategically deploys silence during negotiations. We witness instances where Buffett's deliberate pauses prompted counterparts to divulge more information or reconsider their positions. This illustrates that silence, when wielded with precision, transforms negotiations into a strategic symphony. "In the symphony of negotiation, silence is the well-timed rest that enhances the rhythm, allowing for strategic shifts and favorable outcomes."

Explore the nuances of leveraging silence in negotiations, understanding that it goes beyond mere quietude. We unveil the art of the strategic pause, demonstrating how a well-timed moment of silence can create a space where the counterpart feels compelled to fill the void. This psychological technique prompts concessions, as individuals may reveal more than intended or reassess their stance in the absence of immediate responses. "Silence is not a void to be filled; it's a strategic space that invites introspection and encourages the counterpart to reveal valuable insights."

Negotiators strategically employed silence, can lead counterparts to make concessions they may not have considered otherwise. The pregnant pause, pregnant with unspoken potential, becomes a catalyst for influencing decisions and steering negotiations towards more favorable outcomes. "In the dance of negotiation, the pregnant pause is the choreography that prompts concessions, turning potential discomfort into strategic advantage."

In negotiations, silence emerges as a valuable currency that can be exchanged for strategic advantage. Moments of quietude can become transactions, traded for concessions, favorable terms, or shifts in the negotiation dynamics. "Negotiators exchange silence strategically to secure advantageous outcomes in the intricate dance of negotiations, which isn't just golden; it's also their currency."

As we embrace the strategic symphony of silence, let us recognize that it's not an empty void but a powerful tool that negotiators can harness for optimal results. By understanding its nuances, appreciating its impact, and deploying it judiciously, negotiators can transform the negotiation table into a stage where silence becomes the instrument that conducts a harmonious and advantageous deal.

Negotiation as Relationship Building

Negotiations aren't isolated events; they're opportunities to build lasting relationships. Explore the tales of negotiators who understood that every deal is a building block for future collaborations. We'll delve into the art of building trust, fostering open communication, and creating a negotiation environment that transcends the boardroom. After all, in the business symphony, successful negotiations compose the melodic refrain of enduring partnerships. "A successful negotiation is not just a closed deal; it's the beginning of a strategic partnership that can flourish and evolve."

Consider negotiations as a dynamic force shaping the business landscape, where successful negotiators go beyond the closure of deals. Negotiators should understood that every deal is a building block, a crucial note in the ongoing symphony of business relationships.

The Negotiator's Creed emphasizes that negotiations are not isolated events but opportunities to lay the foundation for long-term collaborations. "In the grand orchestration of business, successful negotiations compose the melodic refrain that echoes in the corridors of enduring partnerships."

Negotiators strategically build trust, recognizing it as the keystone that upholds lasting relationships. Trust is not just a byproduct of successful negotiations but an intentional construction, ensuring that each deal contributes to the solid foundation of a lasting partnership. "Trust is the mortar that binds the stones of negotiation, constructing a foundation upon which enduring relationships stand tall.'

Let's delve into the importance of fostering open communication as the conductor's baton in the negotiation symphony. Using engaging storytelling techniques, we unveil instances where transparent communication became the orchestrator of successful negotiations. Beyond words exchanged in boardrooms, negotiators adept at open communication create an environment where partners feel heard, understood, and valued. "Open communication is the conductor's baton, directing the harmonious interplay of negotiation notes, creating a symphony that resonates with partners beyond the negotiation table."

Shift the focus from boardroom confines to the expansive canvas of collaboration. Negotiators who understand the expansive nature of collaborations forge relationships that extend into joint ventures, strategic alliances, and shared successes that ripple through the business world. "In the expansive canvas of collaboration, successful negotiations become brushstrokes that paint not just closed deals but vibrant panoramas of shared achievements."

Imagine the evolution of partnerships as a result of successful negotiations. By narrating stories that span the trajectory from deal closure to enduring collaboration, we illuminate how negotiators sow seeds of growth. From initial handshakes to blossoming partnerships, successful negotiators understand that a closed deal is not the end but the beginning of a journey where collaborations flourish and evolve over time. "A successful negotiation is the opening act of a strategic partnership, a narrative that unfolds, evolves, and flourishes over time."

In the world of negotiations, obstacles are inevitable. Whether it is resistance, conflicts of interest, or unexpected hurdles, skilled negotiators view challenges as opportunities in disguise. After all, in the negotiation symphony, every challenge is a unique note contributing to the richness of the arrangement. Consider resistance not as an impediment but as the discordant note that, when skillfully addressed, can lead to a harmonious resolution. Skilled negotiators recognize resistance not as a barrier but as an invitation to craft a more nuanced and collaborative arrangement.

Explore conflicts of interest as the counterpoint that, when expertly handled, transforms negotiations into collaborative masterpieces. Negotiators adept at turning conflicts of interest into opportunities showcase that the richness of negotiations lies in navigating diverse perspectives, weaving them into a tapestry of shared success. "Conflicts of interest are not obstacles; they are the counterpoints that, when carefully orchestrated, enhance the collaborative melody of negotiations."

In the unpredictable world of negotiations, unexpected hurdles are not disruptions but opportunities for a crescendo of creativity. The negotiation symphony, with its unexpected twists, teaches negotiators that agility and creative problem-solving can elevate negotiations to new heights. "Unexpected hurdles are not interruptions; they are the crescendos that, when met with creativity, lead to innovative solutions, enriching the melody of negotiations."

In the world of negotiations, challenges are not setbacks but opportunities for creative ingenuity. By viewing obstacles as unique notes in the negotiation symphony, negotiators can craft arrangements that resonate with richness and success. The stories within this exploration illuminate how, in the negotiation dance, challenges become the very steps that lead to a more harmonious and successful arrangement.

As we explore the world of strategic negotiations, remember that it's not just about sealing deals; it's about crafting a negotiation symphony that resonates with success, collaboration, and mutual accomplishment. From the strategic chessboard to the art of silence, let these techniques guide you as you embark on your journey to negotiate billion-dollar deals and forge pathways to unprecedented wealth.

CHAPTER 7

THE POWER OF BRANDING

Welcome to the enchanting world of branding, where the alchemy of psychology meets the wizardry of strategy. In this chapter, we will embark on a captivating journey into the heart of branding, unraveling the mysteries that transform mere products into iconic brands. Discover the strategies that not only captivate consumers but propel brands into global phenomena, creating a magnetic force that attracts loyalty and unleashes exponential financial returns.

The Branding Symphony

Imagine branding as a symphony. Each element is a note that resonates with the psyche of consumers. We'll delve into the psychology of branding, exploring how colors, logos, and narratives create a harmonious melody that echoes in the minds of customers. Through the wisdom of branding maestros, such as Steve Jobs and Nike, we'll showcase that branding isn't just a visual identity but a psychological connection that transforms products into legends. "In the realm of branding, every component should not only be perceivable but must also carry a tangible influence, firmly embedding the brand in the minds of consumers.

Picture the world of branding as a grand symphony, where every aspect plays a crucial role in creating a harmonious melody that resonates deep within the minds and hearts of consumers. In this section, we will embark on an exhilarating exploration of the psychology behind iconic brands, uncovering the strategies that transform products into legends, and illustrating how branding is not just a visual identity but a profound psychological connection.

Harmony in Colors, Logos, and Narratives

Think of every component of branding, including colors, logos, and narratives, as a musical note. Delve into the psychology of color, understanding how hues evoke emotions and influence perceptions. Explore the power of logos, recognizing them as visual signatures that become synonymous with the brand's identity. Navigate through the art of storytelling, understanding how narratives weave the threads of emotion and meaning into the brand's tapestry. "In the symphony of branding, colors, paint emotions, logos sculpt identities, and narratives compose the stories that linger in the minds of consumers."

Let's draw inspiration from the legendary Steve Jobs, a branding genius who made each product launch a symphony of anticipation. Explore how Apple's minimalist aesthetics, sleek design, and captivating narratives turned its products into cultural icons. Jobs understood that branding is not just about selling products; it's about creating an experience that resonates with consumers on a visceral level. "Steve Jobs didn't just sell iPhones; he orchestrated an experience, a symphony of sleek design, innovation, and storytelling that etched Apple into the fabric of our lives."

Venture into the realm of Nike, where a simple swoosh transformed into a global symbol of excellence and aspiration. Explore the psychological underpinnings of the swoosh symbol, a representation that transcends linguistic and cultural barriers, embodying themes of triumph, resolve, and the relentless pursuit of excellence. Nike's achievement in branding stems from its adeptness in establishing a psychological rapport with consumers, transforming a conventional sports brand into a pervasive element of lifestyle. The Nike swoosh isn't just a logo; it's a symbol etched in the minds of athletes and enthusiasts, representing the relentless pursuit of excellence."

Branding Beyond Sight: It's a Feeling

In the symphony of branding, it's not just about what consumers see; it's about what they feel. Emotions are the undercurrents that elevate branding from a visual experience to a profound connection. Whether it's the joy evoked by Coca-Cola's holiday campaigns or the nostalgia brought forth by McDonald's golden arches, successful branding taps into the emotional reservoirs of consumers. "Branding is not just about creating visuals; it's about crafting emotions that resonate, creating an enduring connection that goes beyond the surface."

Legendary brands are those that establish a psychological connection with consumers. Successful branding goes beyond product features and benefits, delving into the realms of identity, values, and lifestyle. As consumers resonate with a brand ethos, they become not just customers but loyal enthusiasts, forming an emotional bond that withstands market fluctuations. "In the orchestration of branding, the resonance extends beyond mere sound; it constitutes a psychological bond that metamorphoses a brand into an integral aspect of the consumer's identity."

Skeptics may argue that branding is merely a superficial exercise, disconnected from tangible financial returns. Dispel these doubts by examining real-world examples of brands that turned effective branding into exponential financial gains, from Apple's rise(that become the first trillion-dollar company) to the enduring success of brands like Coca-Cola.

To put it simply, envision branding as a continuous symphony, not just a prelude. Successful branding isn't a one-time performance; it's a continual melody that echoes through time, creating legends that withstand market shifts and technological changes. The symphony of branding, we'll emphasize, is not just about creating recognition; it's about composing a timeless tune that defines not just products but cultural icons.

From Products to Phenomena

Let's journey into the annals of business history, where once-ordinary products transcended their utilitarian purposes to become global phenomena. Examine the narratives surrounding Coca-Cola's enduring charm, Apple's devoted and fervent fan base, and the magnetic attraction associated with luxury brands such as Chanel. Through these narratives, we'll illustrate that iconic brands are not just about fulfilling needs but about fulfilling desires, creating an emotional resonance that transcends market competition. "Iconic brands don't just sell products; they sell experiences, emotions, and a lifestyle that consumers aspire to embrace."

Let us begin our odyssey with the iconic Coca-Cola, a beverage that transcends its sugary composition to embody a timeless experience. Explore the journey of a simple soda evolving into a symbol of shared joy, celebrations, and nostalgia. The red and white label is more than just a trademark; it's a doorway into a world where a sip of Coke can take you through the history of America. Coca-Cola's success lies not just in quenching thirst but in crafting a narrative that intertwines with the cultural fabric of societies worldwide. "Coca-Cola represents more than a beverage; it serves as a conduit to shared moments, the formation of memories, and a flavor that surpasses the boundaries of generations".

Apple, a tech giant that transformed devices into coveted artifacts and users into devoted disciples. To continue our expedition with Apple lets unveil the saga of how sleek design, innovation, and a touch of rebellion turned Apple products into symbols of status and sophistication. Exploring the phenomenon where waiting for the latest iPhone is not just a purchase; it's a cultural event. Apple's allure is more than technological prowess; it's the art of crafting an experience that transcends the digital realm. Apple sells not only gadgets but also creates an ecosystem where users are not only customers but also members of a global community of believers.

Our journey wouldn't be complete without a visit to the realm of luxury, where Chanel stands as a paragon of sophistication and timelessness. Witness the transformation of a fashion house into an embodiment of elegance, style, and aspiration. Chanel's success isn't in selling garments; it's in offering an entrance to a world of refined taste, class, and the epitome of French chic. The double-C logo doesn't just grace handbags; it symbolizes an exclusive membership to the echelons of sartorial excellence. "Chanel transcends being merely a brand; it invites a realm where luxury is not just a mode of fashion expression but a lifestyle."

As we weave through these tales, the resounding theme becomes clear—iconic brands are not merely purveyors of products; they are architects of experiences, curators of emotions, and creators of lifestyles. The allure of Coca-Cola isn't just its taste; it's the feeling of togetherness it evokes. An Apple product isn't merely a gadget; it's a statement of identity. Chanel isn't just fashion; it's an embodiment of timeless elegance. "Iconic brands don't just fulfill needs; they create desires, weaving dreams into the fabric of everyday life."

Our journey through the realms of Coca-Cola, Apple, and Chanel reveals how iconic brands orchestrate a symphony of desirability. They go beyond meeting functional needs; they resonate emotionally, weaving a narrative that consumers aspire to embrace. The red label, the bitten apple, the double-C—these symbols are not mere visuals; they are notes in the melody of iconic brands, creating a harmony that echoes across time. "In the symphony of branding, iconic brands compose a melody of desirability, turning ordinary products into extraordinary phenomena."

Strategy, Storytelling, and Symbols: The Holy Trinity of Branding

Explore the trinity of branding strategies that lay the foundation for lasting brand legacies. From crafting compelling narratives that resonate with consumers to design symbols that become cultural icons, we'll dissect the anatomy of successful brands. Brands like Disney and McDonald's reveal that effective branding is not just about selling; it's about storytelling and creating symbols that become ingrained in the collective consciousness. "Within the domain of branding, strategy acts as the architect, storytelling assumes the role of the author, and symbols emerge as enduring characters that transcend the constraints of time"

In the realm of branding, strategy assumes the role of an architect, meticulously designing the blueprint that guides a brand's journey. Consider Disney, the maestro of creating magical realms. Their strategy wasn't just about animated characters; it was about cultivating an entire world of enchantment. From theme parks to merchandise, every element was a strategic move to immerse consumers in a universe of dreams. Effective branding strategy isn't happenstance; it's a purposeful design that shapes the consumer's perception and emotional connection. "In the architecture of branding, strategy lays the foundation for a brand's journey, ensuring each step resonates with the audience."

Now, enter the realm of storytelling, where brands cease to be mere products and transform into protagonists of compelling narratives. McDonald's, for instance, didn't just sell burgers; it unfolded stories of family gatherings, Happy Meals, and moments of joy. The narrative wasn't about food; it was about creating experiences. Effective storytelling in branding isn't about bombarding consumers with features; it's about immersing them in a tale that resonates with their aspirations and emotions. "In creating branding narratives, storytelling crafts compelling stories that elevate brands to the role of protagonists, fostering emotional engagement with consumers."

Finally, symbols emerge as the eternal characters in this brand saga, transcending the constraints of time. The golden arches of McDonald's and the iconic Mickey Mouse ears from Disney aren't just logos; they are symbols that embed themselves in cultural memory. These symbols speak a universal language, becoming shorthand for an entire ethos and experience. Effective branding doesn't just design logos; it crafts symbols that echo in the minds of consumers long after the transaction is complete. "In the eternal characters of branding, symbols become icons that resonate across generations, embodying the essence of a brand."

Skeptics may argue that branding is merely a marketing gimmick, a facade. To counter this, let's examine the enduring legacies of brands like Disney and McDonald's. These brands aren't illusions; they are cultural phenomena deeply embedded in societal narratives. The enduring success lies not in tricks but in the authenticity and sincerity with which these brands embrace their strategies, tell their stories, and create symbols that stand the test of time. "Beyond the skepticism, effective branding is not a facade; it's a genuine connection, a resonant story, and an enduring symbol that becomes part of the cultural lexicon."

The trinity of strategy, storytelling, and symbols isn't just a formula; it's the symphony of branding magic. The orchestration of purposeful design, captivating narratives, and timeless symbols elevates a brand from being a product to a cultural touchstone. Just as Disney's castle and McDonald's arches aren't mere visuals, they are notes in the magical symphony that etches brands into the collective consciousness. "In the symphony of branding, strategy, storytelling, and symbols harmonize to create an enchanting melody that resonates beyond the shelves and screens."

Consumer Loyalty: The Golden Fleece of Branding

What turns a casual buyer into a brand evangelist? Let us draw inspiration from brands like Amazon and Google, we'll showcase that loyalty is not just a transactional outcome; it's a journey of shared values, reliability, and a promise delivered consistently on the currency of trust.

The promise of timely deliveries, hassle-free returns, and customer-centric policies became the bedrock of Amazon's relationship with its customers. Cultivating trust involves not relying solely on grand gestures but building it through many reliable transactions, constructing the castle of loyalty in the kingdom of brands with enduring bricks of trust, each transaction a testament to reliability.

Now, let's journey to the North Star of branding—consistency. Google, the omnipresent search engine giant, didn't earn loyalty through sporadic brilliance; it did so by consistently delivering relevant and reliable search results. In branding, consistency is the compass that guides customers through the tumultuous seas of choices. It's not about occasional flashes of excellence; it's about the predictability of quality and experience that consumers can rely on, time after time. "The North Star in branding is consistency, which guides customers through the vast realm of choices." Beyond trust and consistency lies the heart of consumer loyalty—emotional resonance. Consider Apple, a brand that transcends products and becomes a lifestyle. Apple's success isn't just about innovative technology; it's about the emotional connection users feel with the brand. Whether through sleek designs, captivating advertisements, or the anticipation surrounding product launches, Apple has mastered the art of forging emotional bonds. Loyalty isn't a rational transaction; it's a heartstring that brands pluck, creating a symphony of emotions that resonates with their audience. "In the core of consumer loyalty, emotions orchestrate the tune that metamorphoses a brand from a mere choice into a cherished companion."

Skeptics might argue that loyalty is merely a byproduct of discounts or transactional perks. However, the tales of Amazon, Google, and Apple paint a different narrative. Loyalty, in the realm of these giants, is not a fleeting outcome of a sale, but a journey that transcends transactions. It's a testament to the enduring relationships forged through trust, the constancy of experience, and the emotional depth that resonates beyond the allure of discounts. "Authentic loyalty does not arise from momentary discounts but originates from the lasting principles of trust, consistency, and emotional engagement." The quest for consumer loyalty is epic, with brands as the heroes and customers as the cherished companions. Trust, consistency, and emotional resonance become the weapons, the armor, and the magical spells that brands wield to navigate the labyrinth of consumer choices. Like the Golden Fleece, loyalty is elusive but attainable, waiting to be captured by those who embark on the noble quest with sincerity, integrity, and an unwavering commitment to the consumer's heart.

Taking Brands Beyond Borders

Join us as we explore how brands transcend geographical boundaries, becoming cultural phenomena that resonate worldwide. By showcasing the global triumphs of brands like Nike, Starbucks, and Adidas, we'll show how the universal branding language communicates aspirations, values, and emotions. In this era of interconnectedness, we'll unravel the strategies that propel brands into international stardom, making them not just products but cultural touchstones. "In the worldwide stage of branding, although languages may vary, the reverberation of iconic brands makes up a universally comprehensible symphony"

Consider Nike, the embodiment of global sporting prowess. The iconic swoosh, a symbol recognized from

Beijing to Boston, illustrates the power of a brand transcending linguistic barriers. Nike didn't just sell shoes; it sold dreams of victory, aspirations for greatness, and the universal language of pushing one's limits. The brand's resonance goes beyond products; it taps into the shared human desire for excellence, making it a global beacon of inspiration.

Now, envision Starbucks, the coffee giant that turned a daily ritual into a global cultural experience. From Tokyo to London, Starbucks isn't just a place to grab coffee; it's a sanctuary of connection and community. The brand's success lies not just in brewing beverages but in crafting an ambiance that transcends borders. Starbucks transformed coffee into an international language of camaraderie, making it a cultural ambassador that speaks to the desire for shared moments and meaningful connections. "Within the worldwide coffeehouse landscape, Starbucks goes beyond beverage service; it cultivates a global culture of connection that reverberates across borders"

Let's stride over to Adidas, a brand that dances effortlessly across continents. Adidas didn't conquer the global stage merely by selling sportswear; it did so by tapping into the rhythm of cultural expression. From the streets of New York to the soccer fields of Rio de Janeiro, Adidas became a symbol of style, athleticism, and self-expression. The brand's success lies not just in products, but in aligning with the universal desire for identity and individuality. In this era of interconnectedness, the strategies that propel brands to international stardom are as diverse as the cultures they embrace. The language might differ, but the resonance of iconic brands is a universal symphony that everyone understands. The strategies involve more than marketing; they encompass understanding and embracing the aspirations, values, and emotions that resonate globally. "Success in the global arena of branding requires speaking the universal language of aspirations, values, and emotions."

Some may argue that cultural differences present insurmountable barriers. However, the stories of Nike, Starbucks, and Adidas defy such skepticism. They prove that while language and customs might vary, the core human desires for excellence, connection, and self-expression are universal. Brands that recognize and celebrate these shared aspirations become cultural ambassadors, creating a resonance that bridges the gaps between nations. "In the global symphony of branding, cultural differences are not barriers; they are notes that contribute to the richness of the melody." The global theater of branding invites brands to become cultural constellations that shine brightly across the world's canvas. Nike, Starbucks, and Adidas illuminate the path, showcasing that when brands align with universal aspirations, values, and emotions, they become more than products—they become enduring symbols that transcend borders, languages, and cultural nuances. The global stage awaits those brands that dare to speak the language of the heart, creating a cultural resonance that echoes across continents.

Navigating Skepticism

It is possible to argue that branding is an extravagance, an illusion that doesn't translate into financial returns. "In the business arena, skepticism about branding is not a debate; it's an oversight of the financial symphony that effective branding can orchestrate. They argue that branding is a frivolous expense, an embellishment on the balance sheet that doesn't correlate with financial success. However, let's step into the success story of Apple. Once a challenger in the tech arena, Apple transformed into a global juggernaut, not solely because of its products, but because of its brand. The iconic Apple logo became a symbol of innovation, quality, and, yes, financial success. Apple didn't just sell products; it sold an experience, turning skepticism into undeniable financial returns. "In the realm of branding, Apple's success isn't just about gadgets; it's about turning an emblem into a symbol of innovation that translates into financial triumph."

Examine the tale of Coca-Cola. Coca-Cola isn't just a beverage; it's a global icon. The red and white logo doesn't merely represent a sugary drink; it embodies joy, nostalgia, and a timeless appeal. The illusion, in this case, isn't smoke but the magic that turns a beverage into a cultural phenomenon, resulting in financial gains that echo through the ages. Nike invested not just in shoes and sportswear but in building a brand that symbolizes victory, aspiration, and excellence. The swoosh isn't just a logo; it's a financial beacon that attracts consumers globally. "In the financial symphony, Nike's swoosh is not just a symbol; it's a note that resonates with consumers, translating into financial returns that surpass the skeptics' doubts."

Skepticism about branding isn't a debate; it's an oversight of the financial symphony that effective branding can orchestrate. Apple, Coca-Cola, and Nike stand as living testaments to the fact that branding isn't an extravagance or an illusion; it's a strategic investment that yields tangible and lasting financial returns. As we debunk these myths, the curtain rises on an overture to financial triumph, where effective branding takes center stage, transforming skepticism into a standing ovation for the undeniable impact it has on the financial performance of businesses. "In the business arena, skepticism about branding isn't a debate; it's an oversight of the financial symphony that effective branding can orchestrate, turning skeptics into believers of the undeniable impact on financial returns."

The Branding Symphony

In this section, we'll introduce the concept of the branding symphony — a prelude to financial triumph. By aligning branding with financial success, we'll illustrate that iconic brands don't just command market share; they command the hearts, minds, and wallets of consumers worldwide. The branding symphony, we'll emphasize, is not just about creating recognition; it's about composing a melody that resonates across generations, creating a timeless allure that defines financial triumph. "The branding symphony is not just a prelude; it's the ongoing melody that echoes through time, defining not just products but legends."

Consider the legacy of Disney, an empire built not just on animated characters but on the orchestration of a branding symphony that resonates across generations. The iconic Disney logo isn't merely a visual identity; it's a timeless symbol of magic, imagination, and family entertainment. The branding symphony here isn't a one-time performance; it's an ongoing melody that defines not just the success of Disney as a company but the creation of legends that withstand the test of time. Let's pivot to the realm of luxury brands like Chanel, where the interplay of branding elements isn't just about selling products but about creating a timeless allure. The interlocking C's of Chanel aren't merely letters; they're a symbol of elegance, sophistication, and status. The branding symphony, in this context, isn't a mere overture; it's an ongoing masterpiece that weaves a narrative of timeless allure, attracting consumers who aspire not just to own a product but to be part of a legacy. "In the world of luxury, the branding symphony isn't a prelude; it's a perpetual masterpiece that crafts not just products but a timeless allure, inviting consumers into a legacy of elegance and sophistication."

Now, let's bring our symphony to a crescendo with the global resonance of brands like Google. Beyond being a search engine, Google has become synonymous with information, innovation, and reliability. The branding symphony it conducts isn't confined to the digital realm; it's a universal melody that defines financial triumph. The financial success of Google isn't just a result of its algorithms; it's a testament to the ongoing branding symphony that transforms it from a company into a cultural touchstone. It is important to understand that the branding symphony isn't a prelude confined to introducing a brand; it's an ongoing melody, an ever-evolving composition that defines financial triumph. From Disney's enchanting legacy to Chanel's timeless allure and Google's global resonance, the branding symphony is not just about creating recognition; it's about crafting legends, weaving narratives, and composing melodies that echo through generations, ensuring that financial triumph isn't just a fleeting moment but an enduring symphony of success. "The branding symphony is not just a prelude; it's the ongoing melody that echoes through time, defining not just products but legends."

Welcome to the magical realm where strategy, storytelling, and symbols converge to create brands that don't just make billions, but leave an indelible mark on the world.

CHAPTER 8

Adaptability in a changing world

Welcome, dear reader, to a chapter that unfurls the sails of adaptability in the vast sea of business. Imagine your business as a ship navigating unpredictable waters, where economic tides, technological currents, and global winds are in constant flux. In this dynamic voyage, we'll delve into the importance of adaptability, the compass guiding successful entrepreneurs through the fast-paced, ever-changing business environment.

The Resilient Navigator: A Lesson from Jeff Bezos

Let's start our journey with a tale from the e-commerce titan, Jeff Bezos. Picture Amazon as a ship, initially anchored in the book-selling cover. As the seas of technology and consumer behavior evolved, Bezos, the resilient navigator, didn't cling to the safety of familiar shores. Instead, he adapted, expanding Amazon's horizons into a vast marketplace. The adaptability of Amazon didn't just weather the storms; it transformed challenges into opportunities." In the realm of business, adaptability serves as the compass that not only directs you appropriately but also empowers you to confidently navigate unexplored territories".

Our fearless captain, Jeff Bezos, displayed a resilience akin to a seasoned mariner facing the tempest head-on. Instead of clinging desperately to the familiarity of the book-selling cover, he gazed into the horizon with an adventurous spirit. With the adaptability of a true navigator, he expanded Amazon's horizons, transforming it into a vast marketplace that encompassed everything from A to Z.

As the tides of technology and consumer whims shifted, Amazon didn't merely weather the storms; it danced on the waves of challenges, turning adversity into opportunities. This transformation wasn't a mere course correction; it was a symphony of adaptability, orchestrating new ventures, services, and ventures that propelled Amazon to the forefront of the digital retail age. "In the dynamic rhythm of business, adaptability goes beyond steering clear of disasters; it involves transforming unforeseeable currents into a choreography of success."

It is possible to argue that such adaptability is risky—a perilous journey into the unknown. However, the story of Amazon under Bezos' leadership refutes this notion. Adaptability, in this context, is not a reckless venture; it's a strategic response to the changing winds of commerce. It's not about blindly navigating but leveraging the winds of change to propel the ship forward. "In the business saga, adaptability is not the storm; it's the sail that catches the winds of change, transforming challenges into the very force that drives you ahead."

So, fellow sailors, let the tale of Jeff Bezos be a guiding star on our business odyssey. As we navigate the uncharted waters of innovation and evolution, let adaptability be our compass, our astrolabe, and our sail.

In the vast sea of business, it's not the destination but the journey—with adaptability as our trusted shipmate—that defines our success. "In the ever-changing business environment, adaptability surpasses being a virtue; accomplishments rather than setbacks mark it functions as the guiding compass leading us toward unexplored horizons, guaranteeing that our journey"

Embracing the Winds of Change: The Apple Revolution

Now, let's set sail to the land of innovation with a story from Apple. Remember the era of bulky desktop computers? Apple, under Steve Jobs' visionary leadership, embraced the winds of change. The iPod, iPhone, and iPad weren't just products; they were sails catching the gusts of technological advancement. Apple's adaptability transformed them from a computer company into a global tech trendsetter.

Cast your mind back to the days when desktop computers were behemoths occupying our office spaces. In this era, Apple, led by the luminary captain Steve Jobs, stood at the helm, ready to embrace the winds of change. The iPod, iPhone, and iPad emerged not as mere gadgets but as sails that eagerly caught the gusts of technological advancement. "In the business journey, adaptability is more than navigating through storms; it involves harnessing the winds of change to transform disruption into a competitive advantage"

A once-computer-centric company altering its course to become a global tech trendsetter. Apple's adaptability wasn't a mere reaction to the turbulent seas of innovation; it was a proactive navigation strategy. Steve Jobs, with the precision of a primary mariner, didn't fear the storm of change; he hoisted the sails of innovation, steering Apple into uncharted waters. "In the symphony of business evolution, adaptability is the melody that transforms disruption into a harmonious composition of competitive advantage."

Some may argue that such radical shifts bring unnecessary risks. However, the story of Apple under Steve Jobs' leadership debunks this notion. Adaptability here isn't a perilous leap; it's a deliberate choice to ride the waves of change, transforming potential risks into navigational victories. "In the narrative of business, a reluctance to change does not characterize adaptability; rather, it embodies the boldness to embark on a journey toward new technological frontiers, leaving conventional shores far behind"

My fellow sailors, let the Apple revolution be a guiding star in our voyage through the uncharted waters of innovation. As we navigate the seas of change, let adaptability be our compass, our sail, and our course. For in the dynamic ocean of business, it's not just about avoiding storms; it's about dancing with the winds of change, turning disruption into the very force that propels us toward new frontiers. "In the constantly changing business landscape, adaptability is not merely a commendable trait; it functions as the guiding compass leading us towards new horizons, ensuring that successes define our journey rather than failures"

Navigating Economic Seas: Lessons from the 2008 Financial Crisis

As we sail into economic waters, let's navigate the turbulent seas of the 2008 financial crisis. Companies like Netflix, born from the crisis, didn't cower; they adapted, with the rise of streaming, Netflix transformed from a DVD rental service into an entertainment powerhouse. The lesson here is clear—during economic storms, adaptability isn't just a lifeboat; it's a strategy that propels you forward when others are anchored in fear. "In the financial seas, adaptability isn't just about weathering the storm; it's about riding the waves and turning adversity into advantage."

Netflix's journey is more than a success story; it's a testament to the transformative power of adaptability. When others clung to the safety of traditional business models, Netflix embraced innovation. Streaming became their flagship, and in the wake of economic turmoil, they sailed past competitors anchored in fear. "In the symphony of financial resilience, adaptability is the melody that transforms adversity into a triumphant composition, turning challenges into opportunities." Netflix's saga stands as proof that adaptability is not a rarity but a strategic choice. When economic storms rage, adaptability becomes the compass, guiding companies away from the treacherous rocks of stagnation.

My resilient crew, let Netflix's journey be our guiding star as we sail through the unpredictable economic waters. During times of adversity, let adaptability be our ally, our strategy, and our wind-filled sail. For in the ever-changing currents of the business sea, it's not just about weathering the storm; it's about dancing with the waves, turning challenges into opportunities, and steering toward new horizons. "In the economic symphony, adaptability is not just a response; it's the bold melody that transforms adversity into a triumphant crescendo, echoing through the annals of business history."

The Global Navigation System

Our journey wouldn't be complete without addressing the global current reshaping industries. Consider the rise of remote work in response to the COVID-19 pandemic. Companies that swiftly embraced adaptable work models didn't just survive; they thrived. The adaptability to remote work became a global navigation system, steering businesses through unprecedented challenges.

Fellow navigators! Our maritime odyssey takes a global turn as we sail into the uncharted waters of the COVID-19 pandemic, where the winds of change swept across industries, reshaping the very fabric of business. In this tumultuous sea, our focus turns to the adaptability of companies that didn't just weather the storm; they hoisted their sails to catch the gusts of transformation.

Imagine the world as a vast, interconnected ocean, and the pandemic as a powerful tempest threatening to capsize traditional work models. Amid this turmoil, companies that swiftly embraced adaptable work models became the navigators of change. This is not just a tale of survival; it's a saga of thriving against the odds.

Let's cast our gaze toward remote work as the star that guided companies through unprecedented challenges. Remote work wasn't just a response; it became a global navigation system—a compass pointing toward a new business horizon. Companies that adapted seamlessly to this change found themselves not merely surviving but thriving in the face of adversity. "In the symphony of global business, adaptability is not just a note; it's the melody that harmonizes with change, creating a composition that propels businesses forward." The stories of thriving businesses during the pandemic stand as living proof that adaptability is not an extravagance but a strategic necessity. "In the dynamic sea of global business, adaptability isn't just a response; it's the compass that guides you through uncharted territories, turning change into an advantage."

Let the remote work revolution be our guiding North Star as we navigate the vast ocean of global changes. During times of uncertainty, let adaptability be our global navigation system, steering us not just through challenges but toward new opportunities. For in the interconnected currents of the global business ocean, it's not just about staying afloat; it's about embracing change as a constant and creating a navigation system that propels us forward.

Sailing into the Future

As we dock this chapter, envision your business ship not as a static vessel, but as a nimble sailboat, harnessing the winds of change. Adaptability isn't just a skill; it's a mindset—a compass that guides you not just through today's waves but toward the horizons of tomorrow. In this ever-changing business sea, those who adapt don't just survive; they sail into the future as captains of their destiny. "In the business voyage, adaptability isn't just a skill; it's the wind in your sails, propelling you toward new horizons and opportunities."

As we navigate the waters of adaptability, let's pause and envision your business ship as more than a mere vessel—a nimble sailboat with the capacity to harness the winds of change. The art of adaptability transcends a mere skill; it's a mindset, a compass that not only guides you through the waves of today but steers you confidently toward the limitless horizons of tomorrow.

Picture your business ship anchored not in the past or present, but ready to unfurl its sails to catch the gusts of change. Adaptability is the wind that fills those sails, providing the momentum needed to navigate uncharted waters. It's not just a response to challenges; it's the forward propulsion that propels your ship toward a future where you're not just a passenger but the captain of your destiny.

Let's draw inspiration from the metaphorical sailboats that have mastered the art of adaptability. Imagine Jeff Bezos' Amazon ship, always ready to adjust its sails to the shifting winds of technology and consumer behavior. Picture Apple's vessel, not anchored in the stagnancy of bulky desktop computers but sailing with the winds of innovation, transforming into a global tech trendsetter. "In the dynamic sea of business, adaptability is not just a response to the current; it's the anticipation of the winds of change, positioning your sails for the future."

In the ever-changing business sea, those who embrace adaptability don't just survive; they become the captains of their destiny, sailing into the future with confidence. Think of adaptability as the wind that not only powers your ship through challenges but carries you toward new opportunities on the horizon

Therefore, let the metaphor of your business ship as a sailboat linger in your mind. Embrace adaptability not as a fleeting skill but as the constant wind that fills your sails, driving you toward the future where you're not just navigating the seas but charting a course to new heights. In the grand symphony of business, let adaptability be the melody that propels you into a future of endless possibilities.

Chapter 9

Philanthropy and social impact

In the grand tapestry of wealth and success, there is a thread that weaves not just fortunes but a profound legacy—the thread of philanthropy. Welcome to a chapter that delves into the transformative power of giving back, exploring the ways billionaires use their wealth to make an indelible impact on society, creating a legacy that extends far beyond the realm of financial success.

The Generosity Symphony

Imagine philanthropy as a symphony, where each act of giving is a note that resonates through time. Billionaires, akin to virtuoso conductors, orchestrate their philanthropic endeavors with precision and passion. Bill and Melinda Gates, through their foundation, compose a harmony of health and education initiatives, each note aimed at eradicating global diseases and fostering learning opportunities. Philanthropy is not just about giving money; it's about conducting

Consider the Gates Foundation as a symphony hall where the Gates, akin to maestros, craft a masterpiece that transcends the confines of conventional giving. Each note in their symphony represents a strategic move, addressing global challenges like malaria and championing education reforms. Their passion for positive change resonates, creating a harmonious blend of impactful initiatives. "The Gates Foundation symphony is a testament to the transformative power of strategic philanthropy, where each note contributes to a larger composition of global betterment."

Within the Gates Foundation's philanthropic composition, notes on eradicating diseases and fostering education create a powerful melody. Imagine the global impact of initiatives focused on eradicating diseases like malaria or polio—their notes echoing in the lives of millions, bringing health and hope. Simultaneously, notes dedicated to fostering learning opportunities create a rhythm that empowers individuals, creating a resonance that spans generations. "In the philanthropic symphony, notes dedicated to eradicating diseases and fostering education create a transformative melody, touching lives and shaping a better future."

In this symphony, billionaires are not just random donors; they are conductors who infuse every note with purpose and intent. Precision becomes the guiding principle. Whether it's allocating funds to healthcare innovations or investing in educational programs, the philanthropic symphony orchestrates each act of giving with the precision of a virtuoso, ensuring that it serves a larger purpose. "Conducting philanthropy with precision is about ensuring that every note played contributes meaningfully to the larger composition of positive change."

Billionaires actively orchestrate the symphony of philanthropy, leveraging influence, networks, and expertise to create a harmony that extends beyond monetary value, encompassing more than just financial contributions. By embracing a holistic approach, they enhance the impact of their giving, turning the symphony into a multifaceted composition that addresses diverse aspects of societal well-being. "Philanthropy is a multifaceted symphony where the impact goes beyond the financial notes, incorporating influence, networks, and expertise to create a harmonious composition of positive change." In the realm of philanthropy, skepticism sometimes arises about the authenticity of motives.

Critics may raise questions about whether billionaires actively pursue positive change or simply seek favorable public relations. Yet, the Gates Foundation's symphony serves as a resonant response. Their authenticity is clear in the tangible impact of their initiatives, disproving skepticism and underscoring the sincerity of their philanthropic composition. "The Gates Foundation's philanthropic symphony is a testament to the authenticity of giving, dispelling doubts, and showcasing the genuine commitment to positive change."

Therefore, envision philanthropy not as a fleeting melody but as a timeless symphony. Billionaires, as conductors, leave an enduring legacy through their philanthropic compositions. The Gates Foundation's symphony, like many others, becomes a timeless masterpiece—a melody that reverberates through the ages, leaving an indelible mark on the world. "Philanthropy, conducted with passion and precision, is not just a momentary melody; it's a timeless symphony that echoes through generations, creating a legacy of positive change."

The Ripple Effect: How Small Acts Catalyze Big Change

These ripples of positive change showcase that philanthropy, irrespective of scale, is a force that reverberates through communities, touching lives in unexpected and profound ways. Let's examine some illustration of how small acts of philanthropy create ripples that extend far beyond their initial impact.

"In the philanthropic symphony, every act of kindness is a note that creates a ripple effect of positive change." Imagine a chance encounter that inspired a tech magnate to embark on a philanthropic journey. This magnate, moved by the power of education, funded a scholarship program. What started as a modest act soon transformed into a symphony of impact, resonating across generations. The magnate's generosity illuminated the paths of individuals who might have otherwise been denied educational opportunities through the scholarship program. "The tech magnate's scholarship symphony illustrates that even a single act of kindness, fueled by inspiration, can create a ripple effect of a positive change that reaches far beyond its origin."

The philanthropic symphony reveals that the impact of small acts of kindness often extends far beyond what meets the eye. The scholarship program, initially a modest note in the symphony, became a catalyst for big change. Those who benefitted from the educational opportunities created by the magnate's generosity contributed positively to their communities, amplifying the impact of the original act in ways unforeseen. "The ripples of positive change started by small acts of philanthropy often create a symphony of impact, influencing lives in ways that extend beyond the immediate beneficiaries."

The beauty of the philanthropic symphony lies in its inclusivity. It welcomes contributions of all scales, recognizing that each act, whether grand or modest, plays a crucial role in creating positive change. It's not solely about the size of the donation, but about the intention and the lasting impact it has on individuals and communities. Some skeptics may question the authenticity of small acts, arguing that they might not create significant change. However, the scholarship symphony rebuts such skepticism. It serves as a testament to the authentic and lasting impact that even small acts of philanthropy can have, disproving doubts and emphasizing the sincerity behind every note in the philanthropic symphony.

It is important to envision the philanthropic symphony not as a static composition but as a living, breathing entity. Every act of kindness, whether a grand crescendo or a gentle note, contributes to the resonance of generosity that echoes through the philanthropic landscape. The scholarship symphony, among many others, illustrates that in the realm of philanthropy, it's the collective harmony of small and large acts that creates a melody of positive change, leaving an indelible mark on the world. "In the philanthropic symphony, the collective harmony of acts both grand and modest creates the resonance of generosity, producing a melody of positive change that leaves an enduring impact on the world."

Billionaires as Change Agents

Billionaires, with their vast resources, often become change agents addressing global challenges. Explore the initiatives of those who tackle issues like climate change, poverty, and inequality head-on. These billionaires are change-makers who use their money to transform the world, funding innovative green technologies and creating foundations to uplift marginalized communities.

The Green Crusaders

Some billionaires have become environmental warriors, channeling their resources towards initiatives that combat climate change. Take, for instance, the visionary efforts of a tech tycoon who, driven by a commitment to environmental sustainability, invested in innovative green technologies. Through strategic philanthropy, this billionaire aims not only to reduce their carbon footprint but to spearhead a global movement towards a sustainable future.

Foundations for Empowerment

Other billionaires have established foundations dedicated to uplifting marginalized communities, effectively addressing issues of poverty and inequality. A notable example is a business magnate whose foundation focuses on empowering underprivileged communities through education, healthcare, and economic opportunities. By strategically deploying resources where they are most needed, these philanthropists become architects of positive change, transforming lives and breaking the chains of poverty.

The Philanthropic Visionaries

Billionaires, acting as change agents, move beyond traditional donations. They become philanthropic visionaries, envisioning and implementing systemic changes. Consider a scenario where a tech innovator pioneers a program that supports local entrepreneurs in developing countries, fostering economic growth from the ground up. This visionary approach aims not just to provide temporary relief but to instigate long-term, sustainable transformations in the communities they touch. "In the philanthropic landscape, visionaries orchestrate transformative changes, going beyond donations to create systemic impact and sustainable solutions."

The Power of Collective Change

A unique aspect of this philanthropic symphony is the collaboration among billionaires for a common cause. Imagine a scenario where multiple billionaires pool their resources to address a global challenge collectively, forming alliances that amplify the impact of their efforts. This cooperative approach embodies the idea that, in the philanthropic landscape, collective change is a powerful force that can bring about lasting transformations. "In the philanthropic symphony, the power of collective change reverberates as billionaires unite for a common cause, magnifying the impact of their endeavors."

Let's envision the philanthropic symphony led by billionaires as a masterpiece of strategic generosity. Each initiative, whether focused on environmental sustainability, poverty alleviation, or systemic change, contributes a distinct note to this symphony of positive transformation. The billionaires, as dynamic change agents, use their wealth not as a mere donation but as a strategic instrument to create a lasting and meaningful impact on the world. "In the philanthropic symphony, billionaires wield their wealth as a strategic instrument, conducting a masterpiece of positive transformation that resonates through the world."

Beyond the Checkbook

Philanthropy isn't just about writing checks; it's a strategic art that involves thoughtful planning and execution. Discover how billionaires strategically allocate their resources, leveraging not only their wealth but also their influence, networks, and expertise. Through well-crafted philanthropic strategies, they maximize their impact, creating a lasting imprint on the causes they champion. "Philanthropy is a strategic dance, where every move is carefully choreographed to create a lasting impact on the world."

Strategic Allocation

Philanthropy, for billionaires, extends far beyond the checkbook. It's a deliberate and calculated allocation of resources to achieve maximum impact. Consider the actions of a tech mogul who, instead of solely donating funds, strategically invested in education technology startups. By doing so, they not only provided financial support but also catalyzed innovation in the education sector, creating a sustainable and long-term impact. "In the philanthropic symphony, strategic allocation of resources is a keynote, turning donations into strategic investments that spark innovation and lasting change."

Billionaires bring more than just financial wealth to the philanthropic stage—they bring influence and extensive networks. Picture a scenario where a business tycoon uses their connections to bring together experts, policymakers, and influencers to address a pressing global issue. By strategically leveraging their networks, billionaires amplify their impact, creating collaborative solutions that go beyond what individual contributions can achieve. "In the philanthropic dance, leveraging networks and influence is a skillful move, creating a collaborative harmony that resonates across sectors and industries."

Beyond writing checks, billionaires contribute their expertise as a strategic asset. Imagine a scenario where a successful entrepreneur, rather than just providing financial support, mentors and social entrepreneurs - by sharing their business acumen, they empower others to create sustainable solutions. This strategic use of expertise ensures that philanthropy isn't just a one-time contribution, but a catalyst for continuous, positive change. "In the philanthropic symphony, expertise is a dynamic instrument, contributing to the composition of sustainable solutions and impactful change."

The hallmark of billionaire philanthropy is the intentional pursuit of impact. Consider a scenario where a billionaire environmentalist strategically supports initiatives that address the root causes of environmental degradation. Their approach goes beyond reactive giving, aiming for systemic change that creates a sustainable and enduring impact on the environment. This strategic intent ensures that every philanthropic move is a well-thought note in the symphony of positive change. "In the philanthropic dance, maximizing impact is the rhythm, guiding billionaires to orchestrate intentional and strategic moves that resonate with lasting change."

Billionaire philanthropy is not just a passive act of writing checks, but a dynamic and strategic dance. Every move, whether leveraging networks, sharing expertise, or maximizing impact, is a carefully choreographed step in the philanthropic symphony. By mastering the art of strategic giving, billionaires create a lasting impact that reverberates through the world—a symphony beyond checks, resonating with positive change.

The Joy of Giving

Dive into the philanthropic symphony as we explore the uplifting quotes and perspectives of billionaires who find profound joy in giving. From Warren Buffett, who sees philanthropy as a celebration of life, to Mark Zuckerberg, who views it as an opportunity to empower others, these insights offer a glimpse into the immense joy that billionaires derive from making a meaningful difference in the world. In the philanthropic journey, joy isn't merely a byproduct; it's the heartbeat that accompanies every act of giving

Warren Buffett: A Celebration of Life through Philanthropy

Warren Buffett, often hailed as the Oracle of Omaha, brings a unique perspective to philanthropy. He perceives the act of giving not as a duty but as a celebration of life. Picture Buffett orchestrating a symphony of charitable contributions, where each note is a celebration of the opportunities life has afforded him. Through his joyous approach to philanthropy, he encourages others to join the celebration, fostering a culture of giving that transcends financial success. "For Warren Buffett, philanthropy is not an obligation; it's a jubilant celebration of the goodness that life offers."

Mark Zuckerberg: Empowering Others as a Source of Joy

Mark Zuckerberg, the visionary behind Facebook, sees philanthropy as a powerful means of empowerment. His perspective reflects the joy derived from enabling others to pursue their aspirations. Imagine the joyous ripple effect as Zuckerberg channels his resources into initiatives that uplift and empower individuals and communities. In this philanthropic dance, joy becomes the driving force that fuels a virtuous cycle of positive change. "In Mark Zuckerberg's philanthropic narrative, joy is found in the empowerment of others, creating a harmonious interplay of giving and receiving."

Oprah Winfrey: Joy in Creating Opportunities

Enter the philanthropic stage with Oprah Winfrey, an icon known for her transformative impact. Oprah envisions joy in creating opportunities, particularly for those who face adversity. Her words resonate as she describes the joy that accompanies the opening of doors and the forging of paths for others. The philanthropic landscape becomes a canvas where joy is not a fleeting emotion but a constant presence, painting a brighter future for those in need. "In Oprah's philanthropic narrative, joy is the brushstroke that paints opportunities, creating a masterpiece of positive change."

Elon Musk: Joy in Pushing Boundaries for Humanity

Elon Musk, the trailblazing entrepreneur, extends his boundary-pushing ethos into philanthropy. He finds joy in utilizing his resources to propel humanity forward, addressing challenges that extend beyond the confines of traditional problem-solving. Musk's perspective adds a dynamic note to the philanthropic symphony, where joy is discovered not just in conventional giving but in the audacity to dream big and tackle global issues. "For Elon Musk, philanthropy is a joyous expedition into uncharted territories, pushing boundaries for the betterment of humanity."

Bill and Melinda Gates: Joy in Tackling Global Challenges

The Gates duo, Bill and Melinda, form a philanthropic powerhouse with a vision to tackle global challenges. Their joy emanates from the impact achieved in addressing complex issues like health, education, and poverty. Through their foundation, the Gateses illustrate that joy in philanthropy is amplified when strategic efforts result in tangible and far-reaching transformations on a global scale. "In the philanthropic journey of Bill and Melinda Gates, joy is discovered in the collective endeavor to address and overcome pressing global challenges."

Let us envision philanthropy not only to give back but as a joyous symphony where billionaires find fulfillment and happiness. The philanthropic journey becomes a celebration, an empowerment, an opportunity, and a joyful expedition, echoing the harmonious resonance of philanthropic joy that transcends financial success and leaves an enduring legacy of positive change.

Legacy beyond Wealth

As we conclude this chapter, reflect on the notion that philanthropy is the bridge between success and significance. Billionaires, through their acts of giving, create a legacy that extends beyond the accumulation of wealth. Their impact on society becomes a testament to the belief that true success is measured not only by financial milestones but also by the positive change one brings to the world.

In the grand symphony of wealth, success, and philanthropy, billionaires don't just play the notes of prosperity; they become the composers of a legacy that reverberates through time. Picture this symphony as an orchestration of success, where financial milestones harmonize with the meaningful chords of philanthropy. The billionaires, as conductors of this symphony, craft a composition that transcends personal accomplishments and resonates as a timeless masterpiece.

Andrew Carnegie: A Philanthropic Maestro

Consider the historical note of Andrew Carnegie, an industrial magnate who dedicated his wealth to the establishment of public libraries. His philanthropic legacy lives on as a testament to the enduring impact of giving. Carnegie's symphony isn't just about the wealth he accumulated; it's about the countless minds enlightened through the pages of books, creating a lasting legacy that extends well beyond his era. "Andrew Carnegie, a philanthropic maestro, composed a legacy of knowledge and enlightenment, transcending his time and echoing through generations."

Melinda French Gates: Orchestrating Change

In the contemporary movement of philanthropy, Melinda French Gates stands as a prominent conductor. Through the Gates Foundation, her legacy becomes a transformative symphony of healthcare initiatives, educational empowerment, and societal progress. The impact of her philanthropic composition isn't confined to the present but extends into a future where lives are touched, and communities are uplifted. "Melinda French Gates orchestrates a symphony of change, where every initiative becomes a note in a legacy that transforms the world for generations to come."

Warren Buffett: A Timeless Overture

Warren Buffett, with his Sage of Omaha persona, adds a timeless overture to the philanthropic symphony. His commitment to giving away the majority of his wealth during his lifetime reflects an overture that echoes the sentiment that true success is about making a difference. Buffett's legacy isn't about the billions amassed but about the billions dedicated to meaningful courses, creating a lasting resonance in the world. "Warren Buffett's philanthropic overture is a timeless melody that signifies the enduring impact of meaningful giving, surpassing the confines of financial success."

Philanthropy is an eternal echo of a legacy sculpted by the generous hearts of billionaires. In this symphony of giving, success finds its true significance, and the impact endures through generations. The billionaires, as composers of this philanthropic masterpiece, craft a legacy that transforms the world and ensures their story remains eternally woven into the fabric of positive change. "In the philanthropic symphony, the heartbeat of legacy accompanies every note of giving, creating an eternal echo that resonates through time, leaving an indelible imprint on the world."

CONCLUSION

Dear Fellow Fortune Seekers, as we reach the final chapter of "Strategies to score your first few billion dollars," I extend my heartfelt congratulations. Together, we've embarked on a whirlwind adventure through the playful corridors of financial wisdom, guided by the insights and experiences of some of America's most illustrious contemporary entrepreneurs.

Our journey has been more than a mere exploration of wealth; it's been a carnival of ideas, a symphony of strategies, and a playful celebration of the entrepreneurial spirit. Each chapter has been a colorful palette, contributing to the canvas of financial mastery. Now, as we approach the conclusion, let's take a moment to reflect on the wealth of knowledge we've gathered and the joyous path we've tread.

In these pages, you haven't just encountered guidelines; you've met mentors and companions on your quest for billions. The entrepreneurs featured in this playbook aren't distant figures on a pedestal; they're partners in your entrepreneurial journey, sharing their successes, failures, and the whimsical maneuvers that have led them to financial triumph. The goal was never just to inform but to immerse you in a narrative where learning is not a chore but a delightful expedition.

Throughout this playbook, we've unraveled the playful side of wealth creation. Making billions isn't a stern marathon; it's a dance, a play, an adventure marked by the heartbeat of joy. The anecdotes have tickled your entrepreneurial spirit, the quotes have resonated like melodies, and the real-life stories have painted a vivid picture of the mental landscapes that breed financial mastery. You're not just a reader; you're a co-conspirator in the grand symphony of financial prosperity.

Each chapter has been a feast for your entrepreneurial appetite, from the appetizer of innovative ideas to the main course of strategic brilliance, and the dessert of playful wisdom. We've created a banquet where every guideline is a delectable dish waiting to be savored. Learning about wealth accumulation has been transformed from a dull lecture into a joyous experience, and I hope the laughter of success echoes through these pages even after you close the book.

Now, as we stand at the threshold of the conclusion, let's reflect on the essence of this playful playbook. It's not just a guide; it's a conversation, a dialogue, a communion of minds. The entrepreneurs featured here aren't distant mentors; they're companions engaged in a casual yet profound discussion about wealth, strategies, and the joy that comes with it. It's an invitation to understand not just the 'what' but the 'how' and 'why' behind the pursuit of billions, turning this into an enlightening and enjoyable dialogue.

This playbook is more than words on paper; it's a journey into the minds of those who've not only cracked the code of wealth but have done so with a twinkle in their eye. It's an intimate exploration into the mental landscapes of success – a voyage that transcends the limitations of traditional advice and ventures into the realm of playful brilliance.

Let the pages of this playbook be your lasting companion. The great minds of contemporary entrepreneurship have shared their insights, and now it's time for you to craft your narrative. The journey doesn't end with the final page; it merely transforms into a new chapter of your entrepreneurial story.

So, fellow adventurers, go forth with the spirit of playfulness, armed with the guidelines and strategies that have been your trusted companions. The pursuit of billions is not just a goal; it's an ongoing play, and you, my friend, are the protagonist in this captivating saga. May your journey be filled with joy, innovation, and the resounding laughter of success.

Here's to your pursuit of billions and the chapters of triumph that lie ahead. Warmest Regards.

www.ingramcontent.com/pod-product-compliance
Lightning Source LLC
Chambersburg PA
CBHW071041290526
45795CB00004B/1261